INSECURITY UNLOCKED:

Thriving in Love and Relationships

A Practical Guide to Conquering Insecurity, Jealousy, and Fear. Learn Effective Emotional Management, Conflict Resolution, and Self-Confidence for Lasting Relationships.

By

Lilla Rose

Other Titles Published by

THE WAY TO SUCCESS LLC

EMOTIONAL SELF-CARE for Black Women: A Year of Strong Positive Affirmations for Modern Black Women and BIPOCs: Better Yourself, Retrain Your Mind, and Silence Your Inner Critic by Raising Self-Esteem!

POSITIVE AFFIRMATIONS for Black Women: 365 Days of Inspiration for Contemporary Black Women and BIPOCs: Each day Reprogram Your Thoughts, Develop Confidence and Love for Yourself, and Attract Success.

SPIRITUAL SELF-CARE for Black Women: Spiritual Guide that Includes Activities to Help You Discover Yourself Through Self-Reflection, to Self-Care, for Black Women Who Have Given Everything They Have

EXCEL 2021: A Complete Guide to Master Excel's Fundamentals and Understanding of Advanced Features Such as Sampling Technique, Business Modelling and Numerous Methods of Data Analysis

CBT MASTERY: Overcoming Anxiety and Depression with Simple Exercises. Discover Simple and Effective Strategies to Overcome Negative Thoughts and Emotions and Cultivate a More Positive Mindset.

BEYOND ORDINARY PERSUASION: Secrets of dark psychology and emotional manipulation revealed. Master the art of influencing others through advanced techniques of people analysis, mind control, subliminal messages, and body language for success.

PREFACE

Written to help you with troubles and pains that come with sustaining a relationship or marriage is the sole purpose of this book. Believe me when I say you will enjoy your love life, and you deserve someone that looks at you like no one else matters. But I will also be lying if I said there wouldn't be some little bumps on your road. The journey isn't going to be smooth always; this is why your marriage needs you to work.

For your marriage or relationship to be successful, the first rule is the intention to stick with someone and the willingness to pay optimal commitment. It is very easy to assume that your relationship is not working out, and sometimes, the relationship has stolen our peace that all we want to talk about is moving on.

While it is essential to decide to try for your relationship, it is also essential to learn when to set your boundaries and know when it is all dead in there. You must protect your heart from too much hurt because if there is one thing I know for sure, it is the fact that no one is worth losing your happiness for. Feelings grow, but while we want to cherish this feeling forever, we've got to accept the fact that it dies too. So, what do we do when one party is no longer feeling the flame? Does that mean the spark is dead, or does it simply mean that we've failed at making it work?

At the time when your mind is troubled, and you want to let it all go. Look back into your relationship and think if it is worth saving; if that little effort is required. Taking a step back to analyze your relationship or marriage will help you a lot. Rather than settling everything at the heat of passion,

how about taking time out to appreciate your journey and learning to see if you want to throw it all out.

It is essential to know that life is not always white and black, and the decision to walk away is not always the best. I've come to realize that some relationships are worth trying for and that some marriages are worth saving. In the real sense, we are not perfect. It is important to note that this book is not to advocate pessimism but to help you work out your marriage or relationship and live a happy life.

Working with your instinct in this regard is the best way to deal with the fear of letting go or losing someone. I've also realized that we are all scared of losing love, for we aren't even sure there is someone better or anyone who can deal with the situation the way our partner has. In all, something is captivating about trying new things and starting afresh. However, do not let this lead you astray or lead you to think your partner is all flawed. Find in your instinct the decision you want to make and ascertain for yourself if that is the best thing to do.

A lot of issues will put your marriage or relationship on the verge of dissolution. What will remain at this point is not how much you have invested in this relationship or marriage, but how far you are willing to go to make it work and how easy it is to understand that sometimes this is an issue and not the person.

Consciously we love the person, but subconsciously we lose them for issues that are not as important as our feelings. How about learning to distinguish your partner from the issue and dealing with the issue together as a team. If you feel a lot

better than your partner, how about knowing that they are who they are and that marriage demands more than enjoying the happy moments? It also requires that you understand that even a bed of roses comes with thorns.

One of the numerous relationship questions answered in this book is the reason relationships are usually complicated. To better understand this question, I took my readers through the factors responsible for complications and why those factors are just there. This book will therefore provide you with an insight into what you are going through in your relationship. While this may not be all specific, it will resonate with your inner mind. This is where your peace starts.

You will also learn that insecurities and jealousy will not allow you and your relationship to grow. What is ironic about insecurities and jealousy is how far we allow them to destroy us and our relationship because we fail to see that it is insecurities on our part and not our partner doing it all wrong. Identifying these two factors will teach you a lot about the current situation of your relationship, and this will help you know the cause of the problem or the indifference you and your partner are experiencing at the moment.

I particularly talk about an essential element in a relationship; Trust. You've probably heard about how important trust is in a relationship. However, rather than providing facts on the importance of trust, I will be introducing you to the amount of discord the lack of trust can sow in your relationship. You will see clearly why you should not allow those moments of doubting your partner and those moments of self-doubt to take over your relationship. Suppose your relationship faces too many challenges and you find it hard to resolve the issue

or overlook differences. In that case, you will learn how couple therapy can help you and your partner. One of the reasons I believe in this therapy is that sometimes, we can't resolve our issues; we need someone to hear us and make us see clearly. There are more than enough therapists to help you and your partner, and believe me, we are all rooting for this to work.

This book contains practical guides and tips to help you overcome the fear of insecurity, analyze the issues, and learn to separate them from the person while finding a peaceful way to resolve them. Ultimately, you will learn to understand that relationship is not only about the cuddles and kisses; it is also about the pain and the willingness to stay there with someone you love and who loves you back.

More important, you will learn to place importance on your self-peace, self-confidence, and self-esteem. What is certain is the fact that some things will not work, probably because they are not meant to be. But rather than giving up on simple assumptions, you learn to distill your facts and see clearly when it is right to let it go.

I believe in enjoying the moment rather than spoiling it while straining our necks into the future. Following this perception, you will also learn to look at the present rather than paying too much attention to the future.

As a lover, human, and someone who wants you to be truly happy, I hope the process of falling in love and remaining in love does not make you lose yourself, and I hope that in all, you find the courage to keep the fire burning because nothing is as beautiful as loving and being loved.

"Marriage and relationship won't always be perfect because we aren't created to seek perfection. However, I sincerely hope that the peace and happiness that comes with being with someone you love even when it is not perfect is enough to keep your relationship or marriage strong for the trials that are bound to come."

In the end, you've got to ask yourself this question: HOW MUCH DID I TRY FOR THIS?

Good Reading

TABLE OF CONTENTS

INTRODUCTION

A relationship is the union of two people who willingly accept each other's fails and learn how to put up with one another's differences. To some, this definition of a relationship might sound too cheesy, but there's much that can be found in this saying.

Accepting each other's cannot mean you understand the other person is as imperfect as you are and so he/she is bound to make many mistakes. There might be times when his/her words might hurt you, and you might rightfully feel indignant or angry. But what about accepting your failures? Is it easy for you to be modest and admit to your own mistakes?

Differences in upbringing might also show that both you and your partner have different communication styles: he/she might be someone who prefers discussing an argument after the water had calmed down, while you may be someone who wants to address any issue that seems to threaten the relationship. Therefore, finding a balance is key when dealing with problems in a relationship, whether they can be considered "minor" problems or "serious" ones.

Insecurity lends itself to the doubts and uncertainties you see in the relationship. He/she is not in the mood for talking much lately? "Must be something I did" is what you wonder. But what if he/she has told you already that it's because he/she feels stressed out and he/she needs some time for himself/herself to feel recharged. Will you happily admit that he/she also needs time to relax or will you continue guessing why he/she doesn't want to talk to you?

Do you like double guessing your partner's intentions, no matter how good they seem to be? Do you think he/she is always trying to hide something from his/her life? Do you think he/she doesn't trust you anymore? It's easy to let yourself be consumed by these ideas. After all, there are many things that you just don't know about his/her day, you don't know what he/she is thinking. But what all of these questions only do is foster more insecurity in you. If you let yourself fall into the trap that the answers to these questions are worth scrutiny on your part, then you will be undermining one of the bases of any healthy relationship: trust.

If you've only dealt with the type of person that's always open to you and tells you everything, how will you be able to deal with a partner that's not secretive, but prefers to keep some things to himself/herself?

Some measure of privacy and respect will always be appreciated in all relationships. Your partner will be grateful for showing respect and you'll be able to see that you also need some time for yourself to grow and develop as a person. Relationships other than the couple also need to be maintained to have a healthy environment where both know they are respected and interested in one another.

In the worst-case scenario, a relationship can even be destroyed if one makes a pest of himself/herself by always checking the other's relationships and by thinking that there cannot be any uncertainties in the relationship. It's all too common to see how a relationship is ended just because someone doesn't trust his/her partner and doesn't respect his/her right to make his own choices.

You don't need to become the one who will destroy the relationship. Avoiding that is possible if you learn how to manage the behaviors that lead to more insecurity and jealousy.

This book is aimed at helping people get rid of their insecurities by understanding the genesis of their problem and following actionable tips.

CHAPTER 1: INSECURITY IN RELATIONSHIP

In a relationship, both partners will feel loved, valued, and safe. This holy grail of good relationship features is ripped down where there is a significant tension in the relationship.

From envy to behavioral influence, insecurity can express itself in several detrimental ways. Your marital insecurity may or may not be rational, but it produces unhealthful conduct irrespective of the rationale.

What is significant is that such insecurity can also manifest itself in health issues afterward, as studies have shown. Here are seven symptoms of security in a relationship and what you should do about it.

Fear of Losing Someone

One indication that you are vulnerable in a relationship is a persistent fear of losing a partner. Relationship insecurities make you feel like you're not worth anyone's attention, and you find yourself obsessed as to whether your partner really loves you, really enjoys sex, is drawn to you, finds you irritating, or tries to leave you for anyone else. That concern is all the more understandable after having gone through a tough time with your partner, where he/she might have lost your trust.

In reality, a set of studies showed that emotional relationship vulnerability was an indicator of sexual frustration. The relationship is lost without confidence. If you're still afraid that you're not going to trust your partner, you shouldn't be together. Trust is the cornerstone of a stable partnership.

Consuming Jealousy

There is a certain degree of envy in a relationship that is considered good. You're in a serious relationship, after all, and you don't want anyone else to ruin what you've set up. Yet there is a phase when this positive envy is turning into a burning fear. Popular signs of jealousy include:

- Cheating on your partner.
- Continuously checking your partner's whereabouts.

- Aggression.
- Manipulating behavior, such as forcing relationships to stop because they make you insecure.
- Being too close or sticking to your partner.
- Spite and pettiness, such as having a new friend or flirting with someone else only to make your partner jealous.
- Envy is incredibly difficult. That sly feeling is completely reasonable when you're at the moment, but it's not worth sacrificing a decent relationship. Practice how to relinquish any hang-ups and construct trust in a companionship.
- Demanding access to personal electronic devices.

One indication that you are insecure in that marriage is your tendency to access your spouse's electronic gadgets, such as mobile phones, laptops, or social media pages. You may be paranoiac, wondering if your partner has been engaging in inappropriate conversations online. Hence, you feel you should be keeping her under check, thinking that you're protecting your relationship by doing so.

It feels a bit frightening at first, but to realize that you can't change your partner's behavior by monitoring them like a security officer will give you a sense of peace. At the end of the day, you either trust your partner or you don't.

You Are Always Monitoring Social Media

Even if you have the passwords for your partner's e-mail or the unlock code to his/her smartphone, the insecurities you have will still show forth. Rather than going straight to your partner's phone, you're obsessively monitoring his/her social media. You can even Google the name of your partner or search his/her exes via social media constantly. That can result in irrational arguments and deeper insecurity.

Social media is a prolific killer of relationships, and the ease with which infidelity can occur over networking sites is amazing. The American Academy of Matrimonial Lawyers estimates that the word "Facebook" occurs in the filings of one-third of divorce cases in the USA. According to a survey carried out by Divorce-Online UK, nearly one in three divorces resulted from social media disputes.

That said, being consumed in the pictures of your friend by a new 'like' or being keenly aware of someone who is having conversations with them is not a real way of living.

Paranoia and Uncertainty about Where Your Partner Is

Continually checking your partner's location and motives can be tiresome for both sides and could undermine your relationship. Sadly, the hardest thing to do when you're insecure is to trust your partner. The soon after you get into an argument with your companion over her true whereabouts, try to tell yourself that if your partner has never given you a reason to question her, you should stop doing so. It is one of the signs of an insecure man in marriage. Insecure husbands tend to exhibit this action rather than wives.

Need for Constant Reassurance

"You love me, huh? Do you want to be here with me? Are you going to be faithful? Why do you still like me?"

These questions are all motivated by insecurities. If you are unsure about yourself, you may find out that you are constantly requesting your spouse's reassurance for validation.

Unnecessary reassurance-seeking by a spouse is a sign of depression triggered by relationship anxiety. Even though some measure of your partner's reassurance is supposed to make you feel unique about your relationship, it should not dominate your conversations. If you feel stressed or need constant reassurance, therapy can be considered a great way of getting to know yourself better and learning to enjoy who you are.

You Abhor Being Left Alone

When you're insecure in your relationship, your worst fear is being left alone. The silence lurks. You'd like to be anywhere but left to wonder. This fear of being alone may also lead you to remain in an abusive relationship, which does not warrant your time or attention. Seek advice or trust a friend or family member who can give you an external viewpoint about why it's better to be alone and learn to value yourself, rather than remain in a bad relationship.

You Fear Confrontation

You might avoid conflict like the plague when dealing with insecurity in your relationship, even when justified because you're afraid that with the slightest sign of opposition, your partner will leave you. You must practice truthful communication if you want to maintain a healthy relationship. It includes bringing difficult subjects out in the open and sharing one another's opinions and feelings.

If you are constantly suspicious of your partner and feel the need to gather details about their whereabouts with questions such as "How long have you been away?" or "So, with whom were you?" it's a strong indication that your relationship is unstable. Work with your partner to develop trust and establish goals that revolve around getting to know yourself better. Your partner can't take away your insecurities, which is your responsibility.

Overcoming relationship anxiety is a solitary fight. If you want to know how to conquer anxiety or insecurity in a relationship, you must have power over yourself. But if you think that you don't know how to avoid becoming insecure in a relationship and conquer insecurity in a relationship, search for external support. A therapist can help you with how to manage vulnerability in a relationship. To understand how the insecurities can be resolved in a relationship, it is important to figure out what trigger's insecurity. Only then can you understand how to become safe and fulfilled in a relationship.

If you're thinking: "Why am I so uncomfortable in my relationship?" and you can't work it out on your own, please seek support. You would never be able to have a stable and satisfying relationship without knowing how to deal with confidence problems and insecurities. Recognizing insecurity in both women and a man needs to be spotted very early to save the relationship.

CHAPTER 2: THE SOURCE OF INSECURITY

To start feeling better and get rid of the awful sentiment of insecurity, we must find the reason for its existence. Insecurities don't just happen. They can be triggered by past events or traumas. They can be buried so deep within us that we might not have a memory of them. Understanding where it comes from is the first step in beating it.

No matter what aspect of your life makes you feel insecure, the cause for it might come as a surprise. Many who feel insecure about their looks will find the root of the problem is from their childhood and their parent's desire for a child's success. Parents may push their children toward unrealistic goals, and the child will develop anxiety and insecurity about his possibilities. This will reflect on something as simple as the way he/she sees himself/herself, how he/she feels in his/her own body and his/her need for his/her parents' approval.

The same applies to relationships. The source of insecurity in love might be in some traumatic childhood event. Children who witnessed the toxic relationship of their parents might develop insecurities about relationships in general. Or a child who witnessed adultery might grow up to be insecure in his/her partner's faithfulness. This is how we reflect on past events and let them influence our present, even destroy our possible future. To recognize where insecurity comes from, we must dig deep in our experiences and search for possible causes. People will often need help in this search from a therapist or simply someone they can trust to guide them through the memories and emotions related to them.

Insecurity can also be based on recent rejections and failures. People who are already insecure, have low self-esteem and are likely to take rejection and failure more negatively. The feeling of rejection will stay longer with these people, deepening their insecurity. Rejection can reignite old negative feelings and will be a confirmation of their inadequacy. After rejection or failure, people tend to retreat, closing their emotions even more.

They will take no comfort offered by friends. They will see it more as an acknowledgment of their nonexistent worthiness, which will enable them to feel even more insecure. Often, rejection will influence other aspects of life and deeply insecure people might not be able to push through the day, their job, or their friendships. If you are rejected, or you are facing recent failures, an important thing to do is give yourself time to heal, and don't close yourself in your house. Get out there, reach out to your friends for support and activate yourself with hobbies and interests.

Insecurity can also be triggered by tragic events in the past. Events such as the death of a significant other or family member, physical and emotional abuse, threats, broken promises, or any other emotional losses that a person has no control over will influence us in the most stressful ways. The important thing is to have someone close and supportive to help you get through these stressful events. A child needs nurturing and an understanding caretaker to help develop the needed coping skills. The lack of help, support, and feeling of safety will leave deep marks on a person, especially during the vulnerable times of growing up. These marks will leave us vulnerable in future events of loss, and we won't know how to deal with stressful situations.

Attachment

From the moment we are born, we have an instinctive need to attach to our caregivers. This is because infants need their parents or caregivers for survival. We start to develop our attachment systems, and outside factors will influence how we develop these systems.

In the 50s, some psychologists suggested that if we want our children to grow up healthy and develop in the best possible way, a loving and nurturing environment is needed, and a primary caregiver who will be the attachment figure needs to be emotionally open and warm. During that time, this contradicted everything that was considered good parenting. People used to believe that a firm, objective guiding hand kept at a distance would make our children develop into strong independent individuals who won't need to rely on anyone for safety.

Children who are deprived of love and emotional stability, and without someone they can develop a bond with, will grow up unable to have a healthy attachment system and will be too needy, insecure, and possessive. The way our caregivers respond to our infantile attachments will determine our future ability to bond, love, and care for others. A person who wasn't in a loving environment with a healthy attachment figure will be unable to open emotionally to his/her partner and will depend too much on his/her relationship.

Secured Attachment System

Whenever you feel threatened, anxious, or upset, your attachment system will turn on. This may be a feeling of longing for home, needing our loved ones immediately, or needing reassurance. In a healthy individual, once the reassurance is found, and the feeling of security returns, attachment systems will shut off. The feeling of calm and comfort are once again present. The secure attachment system comes from our parents' ability to comfort us when we are hurt or ill. Besides comfort, we also need to receive security and emotional availability that we translate into love.

People who grow up with this healthy attachment system provided by their family will have similar habits when it comes to romantic relationships. In a time of need, when we feel insecure and threatened, we will turn to our partner for reassurance and comfort. Once found (provided that the relationship is healthy) attachment systems will turn off and we will feel loved and reassured, and we can return the same care to our partner.

Insecure Attachment System

What happens when a person grows up without an attachment figure who is capable of providing a loving, nurturing environment? Once the attachment system is turned on, and people receive reassurance of a loved one but are unable to feel comforted and safe, they will have an insecure attachment and we can say the system isn't working properly. People like this will have their attachment system constantly on, seeking reassurance for every situation in their life. They will be too needy, possessive, and dependent on their partner. They will also be unable to open emotionally and develop a relationship with a loved one.

The insecure attachment comes from our sense of how worthy of love we are. It's only natural to fear rejection if you are not capable of seeing yourself as worthy of love. In psychology, this is called attachment-related anxiety, and it may come as a feeling of nervousness, loneliness, or depression. This is divided into four main styles of attachment found in adults: secure, anxious-preoccupied, dismissive-avoidant, and fearful-avoidant.

Ambivalent Attachment System

This attachment system develops early in our childhood when our primary caregiver is inconsistent with devotion, love, and the ability to make the child feel safe. It might be a parent who is often not home in situations when the child needs reassurance, a parent who works too much, or a parent with mental health issues. This creates a chaotic environment for a child to grow up in. This environment is the perfect atmosphere for developing anxieties, anger, insecurity, and even hatred toward a parent or a caregiver.

A person who grows up without constant security will have difficulty with attachment. They will seem too chaotic, with an explosive temperament that will often create problems in relationships. The partner will feel confused and unsure how to behave or even help the person in need. People who develop an ambivalent attachment style will demand constant attention but will give nothing in return and will remain on the sidelines, unable to open emotionally and unable to communicate properly.

Four Attachment Styles in Adults

- Secure attachment style: Demonstrated when a person has a positive image of himself/herself and others. People with a secure attachment style find it easy to connect with others and they are comfortable showing their emotions. They can depend on their partners and let their partners depend on them. They can be independent and also seek reassurance in healthy ways when needed. They were raised in a warm and loving environment with healthy attachment figures. This is healthy and is a trait found in most of the adult population.

- Anxious-preoccupied attachment style: This attachment style is expressed when we have a negative image about ourselves, but a positive image about everyone else. People with this attachment style believe they can't get close to others and develop intimate relationships because they will be seen as unworthy. They have a strong desire to get close to people and develop rich, happy relationships but think others will find them unworthy of love. They value intimacy so much that they often become completely dependent on their attachment figure. Anxiousness will pass only when they are in direct contact with their attachment figure, a partner. These people are also often impulsive in action, oversensitive and over-emotional, they worry too much and constantly blame themselves for a partner's lack of response.

- Dismissive-avoidant attachment style: Expressed when a person has a positive image of himself/herself but negative of others. People with this attachment style are comfortable without depending on anyone; they do not need a close emotional relationship. They are overly independent and self-sufficient. They also don't like others to depend on them. They see dependence as weakness. The desire for complete independence will make these people not need any kind of attachment figure; they will hide their true feelings and consider themselves invulnerable to relationship problems. They will often consider relationships not necessary, and when faced with rejection, they will quickly deal with it by distancing themselves from partners.
- Fearful-avoidant attachment style: Comes to expression in people who have an uncertain, confused, and unstable image of themselves and others. It usually develops in those who've had stressful past experiences, such as sexual abuse or some other type of trauma. They feel uncomfortable getting close to others due to fear that the trauma will repeat. They do want and crave emotional relationships, but their fear stops them from trusting others and opens themselves up. They worry they will get hurt no matter what, and they think their attachment figure isn't being honest about their intentions. They often deny their feelings and are not comfortable expressing affection.

Attachment Style Matrix

High self-esteem	Secure	Dismissive avoidant
Low self-esteem	Anxious-Preoccupied	Fearful avoidant
	Anxious	Avoidant

Belonging to one attachment style or another doesn't mean you are stuck with it. Romantic relationships are a great opportunity to work on yourself and transition from an insecure to a secure attachment style. But there might be situations in your relationship that will hurt you and change your secure attachment style. You have to be careful and assess your partner well before allowing yourself deeper connections and bonds with that person. This is why people like to postpone marriage until the initial feeling of "being in love" or "honeymoon phase" has passed, so they are sure they truly know the person they will spend the rest of their lives with.

If your partner is overly critical and focuses on your mistakes much more than on your success, he/she might lead you to insecurity. You might have had a beautiful childhood filled with love and security, but the actions of your partner might disrupt you and lead you into a constant feeling of threat and insecurity. This will cause you to question yourself, searching for your partner's approval in all actions you take, and it can lead to total dependency on your partner. If he/she decides to leave you, this will only deepen your newfound feeling of unworthiness and you will have trouble connecting with your next partner or new people. This is just a model situation, showing how even later in life we are not well developed because situations and outside influences can still change us.

This model is applicable in a positive form too. If you leave an abusive relationship with strong feelings of unworthiness, but your next partner is loving, reassuring, and acknowledges your successes, you might make a transition from the insecure attachment style to a secure one. Allow yourself to see all the good qualities that your partner sees in you, and you will prosper and feel confident.

Understanding the attachment style, you belong in will only help you work on yourself and your insecurities. If your partner has insecurity issues, understanding his/her attachment styles might give you an idea of how to help him/her feel safe and secure, and how to behave around him/her. This doesn't mean you should tiptoe in his/her presence; just be emotionally available and set the example of a good, well-developed attachment system.

Fear of Abandonment

We talked about the importance of a loving, nurturing caregiver who will make us feel secure and safe. This will make a special bond between a child and caregiver, who is the child's primal attachment figure. But what happens when we are deprived of that figure? What if we are growing up without parents or with parents who are unable to be there when we need them? What if the parents divorced during our childhood were disconnected, abandoned us, or even worse, have died?

When we suddenly lose security and stability, we start to experience fear. As children, we are dependent on others for safety and now they are suddenly gone. Fear that comes to replace safety is a natural defense mechanism; it's a healthy survival response. Many people can overcome this fear and continue their lives normally, finding security in new attachment figures. There is still a large percentage of people who will develop a pathological connection to fear and will actively search for similar or identical situations. They will become attracted to people who are rejecting them, are too critical, or are abusive. Your belief that you are trapped in negative emotions or negative behavioral patterns will keep you away from the happiness you deserve.

You will feel unworthy of happiness and love, and you will seek only relationships where you will be denied these feelings. You may not have control of the situation that put you in a position to feel like this, but the control is all yours and you are the only one who can change your core beliefs and shut down the fear of abandonment. Insecurity will lead you to believe your partner will leave you for someone worthier. If the basis of this fear lies solely in your past experiences and has nothing to do with your current partner, you know that you must work to conquer this fear. It is really hard to control fear. Fear puts us in survival mode and one could say our judgment is clouded by this.

Rationality and logic seem far away and unable to reach when we are in survival mode. Fear makes us act based on our instincts. The first instinct when facing abandonment fears to accuse the partner; accuse him/her of not loving you enough, of cheating on you, of showing more interest in everything else but you, etc. This will create ugly situations of arguments and anxiety, and it will deepen the fear and pain you are already dealing with. This is not a healthy way to deal with insecurity. Your partner is only human, and no human reacts positively when being accused or attacked in any way. He/she will react in ways that will feed your insecurities unless he/she is aware of your past experiences. This is why communication, yet again, is the only thing that can make the both of you understand each other. If you can communicate well with your partner before a stressful situation occurs, he/she might be aware of how to behave in a given situation and will help you overcome your fears.

Core Beliefs

Your experiences, especially those from your childhood, will imprint on you and will create something called core beliefs. They are schemes that allow us to organize information and new experiences. They are a set framework that allows us to orient ourselves in new situations. We use them to make sense of our surroundings. Our core beliefs help us predict new experiences based upon our past experiences, thus allowing us to deal with new situations better. But if your previous experience wasn't a healthy one, it will create problems and make you feel insecure about the present and future situations that are similar to that experience.

We will use fear of abandonment as one of the unhealthy core belief examples. If you had a strong bond with your caregiver and he/she abandoned you, you will develop a fear of being abandoned. When you enter a relationship and come to rely on your partner, your fear of abandonment will be triggered. Relying on a partner reminds you of relying on the caregiver who abandoned you. Your brain is trying to help you deal with an abandonment that didn't happen and won't happen, but it is doing so based on your previous experience. As we see in the above example, the present and the future are determined by your experiences from the past.

Core beliefs are negative or positive ideas that you form about yourself, about others, and about the information you receive from the outside world. They can be either positive or negative, white or black. There are no middle ground or gray areas. This is a good thing because it is quite easy to realize what you expect of someone or some situation. Is it good or bad? Will it end up this way or another? Since there are only two choices, it's fairly easy to make a proper decision. The problem starts when your expectations about your partner are constantly negative. You will jump to conclusions that might not be true and your core beliefs will make you insist on them.

If your partner seems distracted, you might start thinking that he/she will leave you soon but the problem might lie somewhere else, for example, in his workplace. Another example of a negative core belief is when you constantly think negatively about yourself. You then reflect negative feelings and situations on your partner. This is another form of insecurity. Instead of being insecure about your partner's ability to love you and be with you, you are insecure about your worthiness and whether you deserve your partner's love.

There are five negative core beliefs tightly bound to insecurities, and together they work to ruin a relationship:

1. Abandonment: A core belief based on loss. It can be either the physical loss of a loved one or an emotional loss when we suddenly stop receiving reassuring emotions from our attachment figures.
2. Mistrust: A core belief that developed in childhood when we experienced abuse, betrayal, humiliation, or manipulation. A person with this core belief dives into relationships with the expectation of being hurt, cheated, and lied to.
3. Emotional deprivation: This core belief can develop if needs for emotional support aren't being met. It can be the absence of attention, affection, understanding, and deprivation of protection. A person with this core belief will enter relationships believing he/she doesn't deserve support and attention, and he/she will also be emotionally closed.
4. Defectiveness: This belief makes a person think he/she is unworthy of love. It can be because of some inner flaw one might have, such as questioning his intelligence or some flaw that leads a person to believe his/her looks aren't good enough.
5. Failure: People expect failure in everything they do. One will feel inadequate to perform certain tasks; therefore, he/she won't try because he/she thinks failure is imminent. Even if they are successful, they feel guilty as they feel it isn't deserved.

To better understand your insecurities, it's important to be aware of your core beliefs so you can take control of them. Start a journey through your childhood memories and see if your personal story has anything to do with the challenges you now face in your relationship. Remember, this journey might be very painful; it may be smart to involve your partner, a friend you trust, or a therapist. Memories can trigger some negative feelings, such as anxiety, sadness, and shame. Be sure you do not react impulsively in the presence of these feelings, as they could become even worse. Don't blame yourself or others for your past experiences, this journey is not about blame. It is about bringing awareness to your beliefs, so you can start the healing process within you. Make peace with your past and move forward into a happier life. Once you understand your core beliefs, you will be able to better assess the situations when they arise and respond to them accordingly. Your behavior will change and you will stop hurting yourself and your partner with your insecurities.

CHAPTER 3: WHY DO YOU RELATE THE WAY YOU DO

My objective, in this section, is to explain the advancement of attachment styles in the right way so that you can look at yourself (and your partner) and genuinely state, "Well, obviously you're battling with that. How you are thinking and feeling promise well." As with any issue, the initial move toward an answer is to approach it with an inspirational mentality as well as a genuine understanding.

To begin with, it's basic that you understand the attachment system's three essential capacities. These are:

- Nearness: People normally endeavor to keep their attachment figure (typically a parent or romantic partner) close.
- Place of refuge: Whenever individuals feel compromised, they look to an attachment figure for insurance, solace, and backing.
- A secure base: When individuals have a sense of security and bolstered around an attachment figure, they feel a lot more liberated to seek after objectives divided from that relationship.

Your involvement with grown-up relationships is mainly identified with how well each one of these capacities was met via parental figures during your adolescence, and how well they've been met by attachment figures in ensuing relationships. No, you can't accuse it just of your parents. Yet, a solid, educated think-back can go far toward making a course for healthier relationships, by explaining where you originated from.

Closeness-Protection from Danger

The security of small kids is reliant on guardians being close and mindful. Indeed, even as children develop into pre-adulthood and youthful adulthood, they depend on their parents despite everything; however, the parent-kid relationship changes essentially. They widen their system of attachment figures thus may likewise depend on some other relatives, tutors, ministry, or dear friends. And afterward, essentially, they regularly look to a romantic partner (in the long run a friend) as their foremost attachment figure to assist them with having a sense of security and to help their inclinations.

However, "closeness" signifies something somewhat extraordinary for a grown-up than for a little child.

Grown-ups are increasingly compelling when using mental portrayals, or pictures, of attachment figures for a feeling of solace. This implies thinking about your partner, parent, or dear friend can give you the feeling that they are genuinely close, which allows you to come emblematically back to them as a place of refuge and a protected base. After quite some time, you may come to recognize such a great amount with specific parental figures that you join their method of identifying with you into yourself, thus empowering you to keep up a feeling that you have esteem and big expectations that others will be steady. Lamentably, the more you battle with attachment-related anxiety, the more uncertain you are to accept that you have esteem or that others respect you. Therefore, you will have more trouble using mental portrayals as a place of refuge to self-alleviate or as a safe base for investigation.

(I will come back to the possibility of mental portrayals later on in the book, since creating them is pivotal to diminishing both your anxiety and misery in the relationship).

Place of Refuge-The Need for Comfort

Kids are organically wired to look to their parents as a place of refuge from dangers.

For instance, numerous small kids rush to their parents for insurance during boisterous tempests or when they meet a comedian at the carnival (which, from their point of view, is a naturally unnerving animal). However, it's insufficient for guardians to offer physical security. Children must have a sense of security and help in their parents' strength.

Guardians who can keep up their emotional harmony do the best employment of this. By not becoming involved with their feelings, they are allowed to have sympathy for their children's encounters directly from very early stages. When children feel that their parents sympathize with and regard their encounters, they like themselves and their creating capacities. As children develop, these guardians keep on giving delicate reactions as an approach to enable them to acknowledge, understand, and adapt to their feelings as well. (Remember that no parent is whole steady or in line with her child. As opposed to being great, parental figures should just be what psychoanalyst Donald Winnicott [1953] calls "sufficient").

Lamentably, not all guardians can do this-at least when they love their kids. Therefore, their children don't encounter a dependable place of refuge.

They don't feel completely acknowledged, and most likely, won't feel deserving of love. They may likewise see their parents (and by expansion, others) as relationally stunted as well as unsupportive. These encounters of self and other people continue into adulthood. Therefore, to the degree that youth overseers were conflicting or inaccessible in furnishing you with a place of refuge, you will probably be worried about the fear of your partner leaving you; or you may very well not seek your partner for comfort.

To enjoy a safe and upbeat relationship, you have to confront your feelings of fear of being unlovable and dismissed, get them, and sustain another feeling of having a place of refuge in your grown-up relationships. It is anything but a simple assignment, yet it is unquestionably feasible. To assist you with confronting and understand this battle better, you should try the following exercise.

Exercise-Looking for a Safe Haven in Your Relationship

How touchy would you say you are to either physical or emotional detachments?

Whenever your partner is accomplishing something outside of your relationship, what is your opinion about it? Is it accurate to say that you are fast to feeling surrendered, dismissed, or just not thought about? Provided that this is true, permit yourself to encounter, recognize, and investigate your responses (for instance, feeling painfully alone or defenseless). Recall that whatever your responses might be, they have their premise in an attachment system that was advanced to protect you from hurt. The force of your emotions is your attachment system's method of getting out. "Hello, I need assistance here! If you aren't here for me, I may pass on!"

If you are lucky enough to not feel especially delicate to detachments, think about what you do feel. How much, would you say, are you ameliorated by a feeling of your partner being with you (or by a feeling of being a piece of a couple) at least, when you are truly divided? Or then again, do you not feel enriched at least, when he/she is near? Think about whether you feel or attempt to feel divided with the goal that you are generally safe from being harmed by your partner.

Set aside some effort to think about situations when you and your partner have been away from one another and carefully investigate your responses to them.

Secure Base-Support to Explore the World

Notwithstanding offering a place of refuge in a difficult situation, attachment figures additionally give kids a protected base from which they can significantly extend their experience. This is significant because individuals are brought into the world with an intrinsic "want to find out about" and ace their condition. When kids effectively get support for this, they slowly become increasingly autonomous and thus build up a feeling of independence, an ability to act from their inalienable advantages and qualities-for instance, a preschooler will inquisitively investigate a new den or connect with a child they don't know on the play area.

To build up a safe base, children need to feel cherished for what their identity is and for who they are turning out struggles. They have to find that anxieties and contrasts in enthusiasm with their parents would all be able struggles certainly worked through.

During this procedure, children likewise find that they can investigate and wander divided from their parents, and still depend on them for both help and acknowledgment.

To the degree that individuals are sufficiently blessed to have a protected base in their parents, they grow high confidence and a quite solid feeling of independence that will work well for them throughout life. They are bound to seek after their inclinations, be diligent in their efforts, and get along nicely at school and work. In their romantic relationships, they will in general feel associated with, and upheld by their partners as they surely seek after their advantages. Moreover, they will in general enjoy solid relationships and can viably arrange social situations. In any case, this isn't the situation for everybody.

If you are involved in considerable attachment-related anxiety, reading these advantages of a safe base might feature a portion of your extraordinary battles, for example, an inability to investigate (or even distinguish) your advantages and interests, and an aversion to communicate yourself with your partner. As hard as well to feel this trouble, you're as of now taking a shot at it just by monitoring how you would profit by having a safe base.

Adjusting Autonomy and Closeness

To recap the past scarcely any segments: Children are inspired to stay nearby their parents, whom they see as a place of refuge. In addition, kids are inspired to investigate the world away from their parents, whom they see as a safe base. When all works out in a good way, children find that they can have both closeness and independence.

Your battles with attachment-related anxiety can cloud your impression of these examples in your relationships and make it especially disappointing to understand what's turning out badly. To help explain this, I will talk about how individuals with diverse insecure examples of attachment balance self-rule, and closeness. As you read the accompanying areas, think about how they concern you, your partner, as well as your relationship.

Preoccupied-Grasping for Closeness

A few children see their parents as conflictingly accessible. It could be because the guardians are unavoidably centered around squeezing life situations or on their own emotional needs. The child's characteristic affectability is likewise a significant factor. Whatever the explanation, children who come to address whether their parents are accessible or not, are incredibly disturbed even by the idea of their parents not being there for them. This is normal for a preoccupied attachment style.

Driven by their attachment needs, such children do whatever they can to stand out enough struggles noticed. These fights, as John Bowlby (1961), the originator of attachment hypothesis, called them, are defined as a hyperactivating system. That is, restless individuals "hyperactivate" their attachment system as their weeps for attention become more obnoxious, making them increasingly furious and regularly causing struggle within their relationships. For example, they may request that their partner help them in special manners, attempt to keep in touch or become effectively envious and possessive.

Individuals with preoccupied attachment need to center strongly on keeping others close, to the detriment of their advantages and now and again, even their qualities. This leaves them vacant, without an encounter of themselves that they like. Rather, they look to another person, for instance, a parent, friend, or life partner, for endorsement and direction on what interests to seek after and how to react to different conditions. Additionally, they are frequently spurred by the outer, picture-arranged objectives, (for example, money-related riches) as an approach to get an endorsement. Tragically, this quest for outer endorsement always keeps them performing, which impedes their inclination acknowledged by an attachment figure. Along these lines, they are often left without the feeling of closeness they long for and without a positive feeling of themselves, and are unequipped to seek after their advantages.

Dismissing-Making It All Alone

While a few children are preoccupied with attempting to stand out enough struggles noticed, others stop any pretense of attempting to associate.

As Bowlby (1961) stated, after a kid's fights go more than once unanswered, or are for the most part reacted too brutally, the child encounters despair. Then, when he/she finally surrenders all desire for being consoled and secured, he/she disengages-endeavoring to deactivate his/her attachment system by closed-chime down his/her feelings and his/her requirement for a parental figure-and turn out struggles very confident. Then, as a grown-up, he/she is probably not going to encounter the closeness that accompanies romantic relationships. This portrays the dismissing style of attachment.

In case your partner inclines toward a dismissing style, you may feel con-melded when he/she divides himself/herself, instead of mellowing, in light of your connecting strongly. The explanation behind this response is that he/she won't risk being let down later; so, he/she withdraws and might turn out struggles significantly more far off. Essentially, when you are annoyed with your partner, he/she is probably going to show up sincerely divided and unbothered. No doubt, in any case, he/she certainly fear being dismissed.

Cavalier individuals miss two fronts. Unfit to follow up on their craving for an association, they are neither self-governing nor equipped for feeling near a partner.

Fearful-Lost in Relationships

Several children grow up with guardians who have their solid attachment issues: they experience their parents as at times sincerely accessible, some of the time terrified, and in some cases even alarming. This variety is both confusing and alarming, and these kids can't figure out how to meet their attachment needs. They don't find comfort in either deactivating (attempting to go only it) or hyperactivating (connecting for both attention and acknowledgment), so they endeavor to use the two sorts of procedures in a confused manner. This makes a disorganized and befuddling pattern in a relationship known, which is known as the fearful style of attachment. In adulthood, their relationships are regularly loaded up with struggle and befuddling elements, as they seek both closeness and separation. As anyone might expect, they are not able to accomplish an agreeable and ameliorating feeling of closeness or a healthy feeling of self-sufficiency.

Exercise-How Well Do You Balance Autonomy and Closeness?

Relationships are a greater amount of a progressing, dynamic exercise in careful control than accomplishing some consistently held balance. Given that, which of the accompanying pictures best speaks to your optimal relationship? Also, which picture best speaks to your present relationship, or your latest one?

These styles are communicated in the accompanying articulations:

Secure Style

- I am open to imparting cozy thoughts and emotions to my partner.
- I enjoy seeking after interests divided by my partner.
- I feel loved by my partner at least whenever we seek after interests independently from one another.
- Even when we dissent, I expect that my partner will, in any case, regard and worth my feelings and me.
- I am open to relying upon my partner and having my partner rely upon me.

Anxiety Style

- I am most agreeable when my partner and I share the whole of our thoughts, feelings as well as interests-when we appear to have converged into one.
- I am slanted to seek after what my partner enjoys, setting aside my advantages.
- I am slanted to concede my qualities and conclusions to my partner's qualities and assessments.
- Whenever I sense my partner being far off, I feel headed to reconnect (for instance, now and then calling or messaging); or I act irately, for example, by either pulling back or being terrible.

Avoidant Style

- I am awkward about imparting close thoughts and emotions to my partner.
- I invest heavily in acting naturally dependent enough to not require my partner.
- I am uncomfortable trusting my partner.
- I am awkward with my partner relying upon me.
- I enjoy seeking after interests divided by my partner.

While doing this exercise, you should draw your covering circles and compose your unmistakable sentences that better delineate your relationship. (People are confused, so it's alright if your portrayal incorporates clashing sentences).

Presently, think about how well your relationship addresses your issues for a:

- Place of refuge: During upsetting occasions, what amount can you rely upon your partner to give you a feeling of solace, security as well as backing?
- A secure base: How much does your partner bolster your quest for advantages and objectives divided from your relationship? How well does your relationship bolster your liking your actual feeling of what your identity is?

CHAPTER 4: JEALOUSY

When a relationship starts, there's a period in which you learn how to appreciate each other. You begin by assessing your negative and positive features and decide you will still be with the individual, no matter the attributes. In this period, you enjoy being together and their continuous attention, but you also start to experience feelings of apprehension when they're unfamiliar to you.

You fall in love, and new feelings start to emerge. One of these feelings is jealousy; it is a natural response to anything you see as a threat, but it's most pronounced when about relations with others. When you think that somebody or something will take your partner away from you, then jealousy and anxiety start to take root. But it is the way you react to those feelings which will determine whether you'll be incredibly insecure or you will trust your other half.

As soon as you experience jealousy, then you have the choice of acting upon your feelings. Feeling envy is natural, and it's part of your inner self, whereby you evaluate the circumstance, experience the atmosphere, but do nothing to react. Feeling jealous comes from external factors, and you choose to respond somehow: you can decide to handle much better about the situation, restraining the circumstance.

To understand the distinction between feeling jealous and acting jealous, we'll have a look at an example.

You're sitting in a restaurant or a pub, along with your loved one, and you see his/her eyes floating to someone you perceive is more appealing than you. Even if you do not feel threatened by that other person, you may be annoyed by your partner's behavior.

This is the moment at which the green-eyed monster could make its appearance. Still, after all, you are only feeling envy: your brain runs through several situations about what can happen if the threat indicates an interest to your partner. If you react to these feelings, you reduce faith in your partner's capacity to restrain themselves; you then hope that he/she will give in to any temptation.

If you don't react to this jealousy and insecurity and recognize it for what it is, then, after all, you are not insecure or jealous; and this can be a sign that there's a strong basis of trust in your relationship. But, if you decide to react to your emotions, then you're acting jealous and showing insecurity and weakness to your partner.

There are different ways you may act when jealous, like facing your partner in his/her wandering eyes and possibly inappropriate ideas (showing your insecurities), providing your husband/wife with a quiet treatment (often without explaining why). Or perhaps throwing a tantrum or threatening the individual that you think is a danger to your relationship. Insecurity opens the doorway to a whole slew of issues, including bitterness, which manifests and negatively expresses itself. Now you have an idea of how to act and feel jealousy; it's now time to take a better look at jealousy and how it impacts your relationships. The first thing you need to realize is that jealousy impacts everyone's life at some point; it's how you respond to it that affects your future. When jealousy becomes a significant issue, it starts to take over your whole life, and all you can think about is what others have that you don't.

Can You Truly Conquer Jealousy?

Trying to understand what jealousy is. It leaves lots of men and women with the query regarding whether they could defeat it or not. Don't worry, there's a way to conquer jealousy and begin to rebuild confidence in your relationship.

The first step to take to overcome jealousy is to acknowledge that you have a problem. Admitting you have an issue simply means your envious feelings are taking complete control over your lifetime; they're so bad that they are preventing you from being pleased with your present lifestyle decisions, including your existing relationship. However, the biggest problem with jealousy is the way that it can prevent you and your spouse from accomplishing your targets.

Then, what you have to do is to establish if these covetous feelings are taking over your life or if they're just your usual run of the problems that everyone else is coping with. So, how do you tell the difference? Easy search for at least one of these hints:

- You spent all your time wishing you had all that others have.
- You're constantly comparing yourself to others and coming up short.

- You can't spend a lot of time with some people since you always feel bad about yourself because you think you are not good enough.
- Have a tough time accepting the fact that your partner has friends besides you.
- Never like a night out with your partner since you feel like everyone around you is far better than you.

Where's It Coming From?

As soon as you are aware you have an issue, you have to determine where it's coming from; this will require you to look deep inside yourself, and it can be very debilitating. You have to decide what makes you so jealous, what happened to you to create such feelings. Understanding where these feelings are coming from is the only hope you've got to know what needs to be fixed in your relationship. To assist you in narrowing down the most probable causes of these feelings, here are a few things you may look in:

- **Material things:** You're jealous of material things owned by others, and this may have adverse effects on your relationship. The reason is that you feel that what you have is enough. You have to work on the way you see yourself to address this sort of issue.
- **Your look:** If you're worried your look is not as great as others, that's going to eat you and your relation away. This will impact every facet of it because you'll never be pleased when heading out on dates and you'll always be second-guessing things. To help solve this problem, you may focus on improving your looks by exercising and dieting, or you can concentrate on reminding yourself you are worth loving.
- **Relationships:** This is probably the most frequent issue when it comes to jealousy. If you end up worried about other relations (friendship) your partner might have, there's a critical issue. If your jealousy of this kind gets to the stage, you want your relations to be like your partner's one. Then it's time to evaluate your relationship to see if it is worth saving it.

The intriguing thing about jealousy is the fact that it's just the individual who's feeling it that will relate to it. Jealous individuals are often confused, and in some cases even afraid of what's happening with their partner; this may lead to starting questioning their other half. Some of the common questions asked by an insecure partner include, but aren't restricted to:

- Am I still attractive?
- Do you still love me?
- Will you leave me?

Jealousy may lead a rational person into demonstrating some exceptionally irrational, or perhaps loony, behavior, which, too frequently, creates difficulties within the relationship. Generally, everything starts when you lose confidence in your partner when you don't believe him/her, no matter what they say.

You will start to follow your partner around once they start calling you to let you know they're going to be late from work, or when they do something which appears to be outside of their routine. Things just get worse when you realize it can be because of another man/woman. You begin to imagine the worst-case scenarios, as he/she may leave you.

All of these are signs that you're feeling insecure and vulnerable as a consequence of becoming jealous and not being able to convey your feelings. Your partner is not able to have any privacy anymore, then he/she will start to hide things in the attempt of letting you feel somehow how it is not to be trusted, and believe me, it's not that they don't wish to inform you. So, communication may come to a standstill. This type of scenario spells the start of hardship in your relationship, especially if your partner is innocent of whatever you might have accused him/her. They might feel deeply hurt that you have such thoughts and behaviors.

Let's face it, jealousy, insecurity, and anxiety all come down to one thing: hope.

Can There Be Trust in a Relationship?

If you're constantly worrying about your spouse straying, you've got trust problems. More than anything, these have to be addressed; otherwise, the future of this relationship is shaky. Luckily, there is excellent news. You have chosen this book as you understand you have these kinds of problems, or you know your partner is experiencing them. But, how do you tell the difference between sensible concern and intense jealousy or mistrust?

If you started tracking down your partner's movement. After all, you are afraid he/she will cheat on you or checking everything he/she tells you because you think he/she is dishonest, then you're jealous, insecure, and nervous. In a healthful and balanced relation, you'd have the ability to ask your partner about their whereabouts, and hope that the answer you get is the truth. In a healthy relationship, you'll also have a reasonable quantity of self-esteem, which might imply that you value yourself enough to believe that you're exactly what your partner wants, so they don't have any reason to ramble.

While doing some detective work, you may get a few fast responses about if your partner has strayed, but it won't offer you the psychological satisfaction that you wished for. This is because if you start fishing for information damaging your liaison, you're guaranteed to discover some filth since nobody is perfect.

If you don't get any negative info, you might misread some information to let them fit in the situation you pictured in your mind. The reality is, you're asking yourself a question which you will not even wish to admit. That issue is, "Should I ask my spouse to love me and make me feel safe in our relationship? Will they do this, or will they abandon me?"

There are various questions that couples will need to ask each other once they opt to stay committed to one another. When coping with jealousy, if you're not able to ask your girlfriend some questions, you'll develop more insecurities, which will just become a more severe issue later on. You have to understand your loved one isn't accountable for making you feel a specific way. You should be honest with yourself, you have to deal with the reasons you are feeling insecure and nervous, and so you can solve the issues that jealousy has caused to your relationship. Doing this will let you set up an active course leading towards complete confidence.

Here's a list of things that you could look for to understand whether you or your partner suffer from jealousy:

- You or your partners would like to look at emails, have accessibility to social networks, undergo the correspondence party with different individuals, or even insist that you should have access to each other's passwords.

- You cannot have a telephone conversation with him/her close by.
- As soon as your partner calls you to let you know they're likely to be late, or vice versa, and you don't trust him/her.
- You're feeling anxious when your love goes out with friends and wonder if they'll meet somebody who might lead them astray.
- You are feeling insecure when your spouse talks with different persons, particularly if they're of the opposite gender.

Although it's healthy and expected that you might experience some jealous thoughts, you need to have the ability to talk openly with your partner about them, that's exactly what will let you conquer them entirely. Communication is essential to establish confidence in your relationship. By discussing your emotions, particularly your jealous feelings, you empower both yourself and your loved one. Acting in your jealousy may have catastrophic consequences; incorrect accusations can harm the foundation of your relationship.

As opposed to acting jealous and focus on doing detective work, or casting your bitterness through accusations, take some time to speak about your feelings with your other half before they start to spiral completely out of your hands.

Strategies to Deal with Your Jealousy

So far, we've discussed how jealousy can affect your relationship, but what we haven't examined yet is how you can tackle your jealousy. In the first phases of a relationship, a more possessive behavior may be welcomed; however, the more your relationship goes on, the more undesirable this behavior becomes.

Many partners believe at first jealousy is sweet; they believe it reveals how much their half cares about them. However, as time passes and jealousy continues, it usually transpires into something neither party would like to take care of. The more jealous you become, the higher your partner will pull off.

Fundamentally, the more possessive you'll be, the more trapped your partner will feel. Now, do not get us wrong, occasionally jealousy can add something to a relation, but everything you have to do is to understand when and how to take care of it so that it doesn't ruin your relationship.

Trusting Your Partner

This one may seem obvious, but it's the most crucial step to do when attempting to take care of jealousy. If you are an extremely jealous person, the odds are that you will probably become suspicious of everything your partner says. But all you are doing is setting up your relationship to fail.

You have to begin taking your partner's word for what it is; it is going to be very difficult to do so. It is not a shift that will take place immediately, but you have to do it.

In case you've been checking your partner up, quit doing that. If he/she tells you something, believe him/her. There's another behavior you have to watch out for if you are trying to trust your husband/wife, and that's stalking. As a jealous individual, it's plausible that you've committed a significant amount of your time to check and assess everything she/he does.

This might be online or, perhaps, you follow him/her into the office to find out who he/she is interacting with. First off, you have been aware that this behavior is forbidden, and you may get into some serious trouble for this. But you also need to understand that this is the sort of behavior that will add fuel to the fire, that makes a terrible situation worst, and it'll be terrible for you!

In case you've unconsciously turned into a stalker, it's time for you to take control of your relationship back, to be ready to trust your partner completely. That is undoubtedly a straightforward thing to take care of; below, there are few measures you can follow that will make it much easier for you to achieve your goal.

Learn to Calm Yourself Down

You are the only person who can have complete control over your emotions; learn how to calm yourself down so you don't stalk someone. When you're about to spy on your partner, remind yourself that what you're about to do will damage your relationship, and it's not worthwhile. Then, stop. Talk to yourself throughout the whole situation and make sure you understand the possible effects of your actions.

Learn How to Talk with Your Partner

The next thing to do is to talk to your partner about your activities and the potential need to check them up. When your partner knows that you may call him/her a few times daily, or you need to talk to him/her frankly about what he/she and you're doing, he/she will probably react positively. If he/she thinks you don't believe him/her and you are just invading their privacy along with your activities, then he/she is going to clamp up, and difficulties will arise in your relationship. Communication is at the center of a successful liaison and can also help you develop trust with unbelievable ease.

Quit Judging Yourself

Among the most significant reasons why people are jealous, there is a lack of self-esteem. Such people always feel as if they are not good enough for anything or anybody. Sure, there will be parents around who have more cash than you, that are funnier than you, but you don't have to be worried about it. Your partner picked you for a motive. You will need to stop focusing on the reasons why they should not enjoy you and instead concentrate on the fact that they just love you.

Never Play Games

This is most likely the most damaging thing you can do in a relationship. Regrettably, it's something that goes on pretty much daily. People are not happy with just being jealous so that they do everything in their capacity to make their partner feel envious.

The very last thing they would like to see is you are flirting with other people in front of them. Lies and tricks will not build a prosperous relationship. You can't do certain things, so you create scenarios and answers that are suitable for you. You can't decide that you're in charge of another person's feelings.

This not only will mess up the little confidence left in your relationship, but it is also going to cause long-term bitterness; it also becomes hard to fix. In the worst-case scenario, this may even be described as psychological abuse. Frankly, playing a manipulation game generally ends up backfiring on you anyhow. The chances are that your partner won't get jealous, they'll just get angry.

At the same time, this does not mean you have to pretend that good-looking people do not exist. Additionally, if things do go sour, your spouse can use these sorts of things against you once the relationship ends.

Quit Mixing Your Imagination with Reality

A feverish imagination can be enjoyable; however, it can replace reality. It is really easy to become caught up in things we imagine in our minds, ending to believe that they are real, and that may affect our relationships. Here's an example:

You're intended to meet up with your partner at an office meeting that starts at 7.00 pm. Around 6.00 pm, you attempt to give them a phone call, but he/she does not pick up the phone. Your heart flutters, only a bit! It hasn't yet become a full-blown panic. But when you call again in half an hour, and still you don't get a reply, your brain begins to run off with you.

You start thinking that he/she is with another individual that he/she won't come to your meeting; you have determined it is the conclusion of your relationship; you are accepting all your thoughts as reality. At 7.00 pm; however, your partner appears and puts you in a suspicious psychological condition. Most probably, all that happened was that he/she was getting dressed, or he/she was traveling to satisfy you personally, but your creativity may have ruined what should have been a great greeting at the end of the day. Imagination isn't precisely the same thing as reality. The earlier you figure this out, the sooner you can begin effectively coping with your jealousy.

Provide Your Partner Freedom

It is not easy to give your girlfriend/boyfriend the freedom he/she deserves. Jealousy, all too frequently, absorbs the whole relationship: you worry a lot about what exactly your other half is doing. You wish you could dedicate every waking minute to him/her to be sure that he/she isn't doing something wrong!

Sure, it's beautiful to spend time with your partners, but every second is like carrying things a bit too much. Give him/her the independence he/she deserves, do not fight him/her when heading out with friends, and when he/she speaks with others when outside together, don't get annoyed.

Freedom isn't just purely physical, but also, sometimes, emotionally. This usually means you don't check on him/her every ten minutes like you do not always check his/her telephones or societal networking accounts. Allow your wife/husband to express himself/herself and be who he/she actually would like to be without anxiety.

Use Your Imagination for Good Not Bad

Today this may appear a bit odd; however, your fervid imagination can help you get a deal with your jealousy. Most of the jealous persons allow their imaginations to run rampant. We picture our partner doing something to damage us, no matter how naive the situation could be. To get a deal on our jealousy, then we have to take our ideas to another degree. Think about your relationship ending, then think about how your life will be after that.

Imagine precisely how your life is going to be, only in case the worst occurs. You might even use your overactive imagination differently. Let yourself imagine every single possible situation between your partner and what you believe he/she is doing. Now place yourself on the scene, but without reacting to what he/she is doing. See yourself becoming calm while he/she is flirting with someone else. Imagine these situations and your reactions many times every day. The longer you practice, the more quickly you will have the ability to control your jealousy.

Your Jealous Partner

So far, this chapter has addressed what it means to take care of your jealousy towards your partner; however, what happens when you're the one on the receiving end of a jealous lover? Trust goes two ways. It has to be said: it is a lot simpler to take care of your jealousy than it is to manage somebody else jealousy.

Here's what you may expect from a jealous partner.

Suspicion

You may always be under the microscope. Your partner will find it hard to believe everything you say. There's nothing you can do. You have to be ready to be under constant evaluation, and if for any reason you do something that's out of routine, you need to be prepared for the backlash.

Be ready for your relationships with other people to be examined and diced in an attempt to catch you in wrongdoing. Even something naive involving you and a relative may be misread. You feel utterly powerless in solving the issue.

There are many points you should remember when handling jealousy, especially when your partner is the jealous one.

The first one is that you can't change the individual or solve his/her jealousy for him/her. It's his/her problem, and you might not be completely aware of where it comes from.

There are several things; however, which you could do to help the situation, and help you to maintain your lucidity:

- Being fully conscious of any possible way you might be contributing to this problem. Start by honestly assessing your behavior in the situation in which you are and ask yourself some compelling questions. The first of those questions should be: Is there anything I have done to trigger my partner's jealousy? Has your loved one witnessed you flirting with other men/women? Even if you're doing something innocent to you, you have to know that it might be considered improper by him/her. You might be the cause of this jealousy, and that means you can focus on fixing your behavior. You might realize that this can make a big difference.
- Treat your partner with kindness and love to reestablish the confidence he/she initially had. Bear in mind that you're probably dealing with an insecure partner who wishes to feel like their vulnerability is justified, and you're accountable for this. As a result, if they could lead you into a debate that veers off subject, then you are going to end up more frustrated, and they wind up feeling warranted. In any case, the relationship doesn't benefit.
- What you have to do is put some boundaries to stop the suspicious behavior of your partner. As you did before, you want your other half to take responsibility for his/her improper conduct as well, through a quiet conversation. Now you should be sure about what you think to be okay and what's not. Talk from your standpoint, and don't make assumptions about what your partner wants. Make sure that you fit within specific bounds;

so that all your spouse chooses to do to you, you can do to him/her too.

- Don't spare your feelings, let your partner know how jealousy is impacting your relationship, and that he/she should find a way to manage it. You have to do this peacefully and without debate, regardless of what response or outburst your partner shows.

At the same time, offer to help your loved one identify ways to overcome jealousy. You have to let your partner know he/she will need to face his/her jealousy and let it go.

CHAPTER 5: WHY DO YOU NEED TO AVOID TOXIC PARTNER

There comes a point in time when you need to cease thinking about what you are losing and begin to think about what you will get by leaving the relationship. This is because the longer you stay in the relationship, the harder it will be for you to get your serenity.

If life was similar to romance movies, the one we fall in love with would be the one to make us happy. However, in reality, things tend to go differently. We fall in love, let our guard down, and someone takes advantage of this to hurt us multiple times. Yes, it is fine to fight for a relationship, but when the relationship is toxic, you need to learn when to say enough. This is because if you don't, the damage it will cause you down the line can be irreversible.

Love can seem like an addiction, and like all addictions, there are healthy and unhealthy ones. Relationships are also the same. And relationship addictions can break down a person in the most negative ways. A relationship that is toxic and filled with emotional abuse, hostility, danger to you, and other toxic behaviors is the most difficult to leave. In theory, they should be easy to walk away from, but practically, this is not the case. And this is why it is essential for you to walk away as fast as possible, because the longer you stay, the harder it is to let go.

Knowing When to Say Enough and Walk Away

There are instances when the signs are apparent. These could range from cheating, physical, and emotional abuse, continuous criticism, among others. Sometimes the signs may be as mild as lack of intimacy, perpetual heartache, and loneliness.

It is hard to leave any relationship, including toxic ones. It requires a tremendous amount of strength and energy to say enough and let go of a toxic relationship. So, what do you need to do to help you through saying enough? The steps we will be covering in this section can be of help.

Stay in the Present

It is tempting to live in the memories of your relationship. For instance, how the relationship used to be. The same applies to living in the future.

That is hoping that things in your relationship will get a lot better or fantastic. However, if you need to find the strength to leave a toxic relationship, you need to live in the now or present. To do this, experience the entire relationship for what it is at that moment. Doing this will help you see how damaged or toxic the relationship you are trying to save is.

When you constantly look at the relationship the way it once was or the way you hope it would be, to convince yourself to stay, then there is a problem. See the relationship for what it is, and it will be less complicated for you to make your choice.

Have a Record

Keeping track of how the relationship makes you feel can be another excellent means of helping you decide. Keep a journal in which you comprehensively describe everything you feel about the relationship. You need to include the day-to-day events of the relationship over a specific period. If you don't enjoy writing, it is also possible to take advantage of pictures to help you with this. Take a photograph of every vital moment in a relationship that brought out either a bad or good reaction from you. Do it for a specific period which could be 1–2 months, or weeks, depending on what is suitable for you.

After the set period, go through your records and answer the following questions:

- Are the feelings mostly good or bad?
- How often do these feelings take place?
- Is there a pattern?
- Is it a continuous or rare occasion?
- Do you love the person you have become?

If you used pictures:

- Do you look happy or lively or drained out from them?
- Do you seem sadder than usual?

Providing answers to these questions can let you view the relationship the way it is. Without the excuses and paddings, you make it more appealing to yourself. In the end, you will see things with more clarity and make the right decision.

Observe What Your Body Says

The mind and the body are interconnected. The connection they both shares is quite powerful. If you block off the messages and signs that your mind or gut tries to tell you, then your body takes up the role. You will observe some feelings and signs in your body like tension and heaviness, among others. Also, the way it works will change.

To determine what your body is saying, ask yourself the following:

- Do I feel physical pain in my body?
- Is there a feeling of heaviness in my body?
- Does my body ache?
- Does it look like I am losing weight?

Providing accurate answers to these can help you see the relationship for what it is.

What Is Your Coping Mechanism?

Look within yourself; do you have any coping mechanisms to ensure you don't feel terrible? Or what behaviors have you adopted to help you in the relationship?

As opposed to not dealing with the terrible feelings that arise, try to examine them. When you deal with the pain you are feeling; you will get the strength, bravery, and wisdom you require to be able to say enough.

Put a Deadline in Place

When you hope for something to improve in the future, it is not difficult to forget how long you have been waiting. To place a deadline, select a specific period, be it a few weeks, months, or even a day. You need to pick a deadline that you feel is ideal for you. During this period, do all you can for your relationship. Put in as much energy as you can into it until you exceed the period you have set aside for yourself. Then observe the results, and you will find the answer you need.

Get Out of Your Role

In all relationships, each partner picks up a role over time. This is more like a pattern that keeps the relationship going and allows each partner to maintain their behavior. This does not imply that you are responsible for being treated the way you are being treated, especially if the relationship is toxic. However, it does mean that you have picked up a particular way of behaving that makes it easy for you to bear the unhealthy relationship.

In toxic relationships, there is a victim, and there is an abuser. You need to determine what your exact role is. Are you the rescuer? Or the one who keeps giving excuses for the other? Determine your role and try to get out of it. By changing the dynamic this way, it will ensure the unhealthiness in your relationship is more apparent, making it less complicated for you to say enough, and leave the relationship. At the very least, you may trigger a positive change in your partner.

Leave the Imagination Behind

When you fantasize about the possibilities of the future, it can result in you being tied down to a toxic relationship. Holding on to fantasies will prevent you from seeing things as they are. Because you believe things can get much better, as you have seen in your fantasies, you will keep trying until you can try no more.

The more you allow your imagination to rule you, the more you try to change your reality to match your fantasy. The same applies even if you are in an unhealthy relationship. Your imagination will push you to hold on longer than you usually should, even if the relationship is a toxic one. If the way you imagined your relationship was going to become a reality, it would have changed already. So, let go of the imagination, and you will see things for how they are, which will give you the energy to say enough.

Defend Your Well-being

By prioritizing yourself, you will indirectly give yourself the energy to fight for yourself. Everyone, including you, deserves happiness, but in most cases, you will have to fight for the joy you want. Give yourself a priority and fight to get the best treatment for yourself in a relationship. When you observe it is not something your existing relationship will offer you, you will get enough energy to walk away.

Stop the Excuses

It is perfectly normal for us as humans to give excuses for those we love. This becomes particularly heightened when we are in a relationship with that person. However, doing this excessively does not make one see the relationship for what it is and can make you stay longer than you should in a toxic relationship.

Search within yourself. Have you ever gotten what you desired from this relationship? How does your desire differ from what you presently have? Does it feel like you are being loved or treated right?

In a healthy relationship, even when arguments arise and we say and do things out of anger, you can still feel the respect and love behind it, even during the hard times. Once you stop making excuses for your partner, you will be able to see the relationship more clearly and see it for what it is.

Unhinge Your Mind

If in your mind you genuinely believe you can't leave, then it will be difficult for you to do so. Do not limit yourself by constantly believing that you can't leave. Change your mindset and tell yourself you can leave when you want to. Make your choices based on what you want, not based on what you think you can't do. By changing your mindset, you will get the strength you desire to decide what you truly want.

Take Courage and Decide

Lastly, take courage and make your decision. And whatever you choose to do, ensure you own the choice you make, knowing you were responsible for making this decision. If you don't decide now, it may seem fine for a while; however, over time, it will keep you tied down, and without the strength, you require saying enough and leave this toxic relationship. Besides, note that if a relationship feels toxic and unhealthy for you, then it probably is. At this point, you can fight as hard as you can to fix your relationship.

However, when you have no more energy to keep on fighting, you will see things clearly, as they are. Every relationship goes through difficult times and can get past it. However, in unhealthy relationships, this cycle is repetitive, which makes it essential to either fix it or leave it as soon as you can. The decision to remain or leave an unhealthy relationship lies with you, but you need to be sure your reasons are the right ones when you do make a choice. If you decide to say enough and leave the relationship, you will need to learn the appropriate way to do so.

CHAPTER 6: REAL-WORLD SITUATION

Couples/partners are bound to face various types of challenges, which they need to address as they progress. Your capability to manage the issues as they crop up in the relationship will help determine the relationship's growth. In case a challenge or issue is not managed properly, you might find your healthy relationship in a phase of the crisis. You might also need to take some serious steps to find your way out of the issue. Some of the most common challenges faced by people in their relationships are relationship needs, communication, developing jointly as a couple, equal rights, contentedness, habit, routine, loyalty, sexuality, fights, stress, value differences, conflicts, illness, distance, and this list will keep going on.

How much care are you and your partner in the relationship? Being considerate and careful can help in avoiding most of the frustrations in your relationship. Are you able to enjoy the moment? Living in the present sounds much easier than doing the same. It might not be now, but sometimes our thoughts from the past or the future will try to slide in. There are certainly other questions that you will need to ask yourself. How much are you enjoying the present moment? Can you make your partner understand what you want to say? Do you both spend a lot of time together doing common things? Can you feel tenderness, sexual satisfaction, and security with your partner? Do you find support and peace in the relationship? Can you discuss anything openly with your partner? Do you feel strong with your partner?

As you answer all of these questions, you will be able to guide yourself properly on the road to self-evaluation of various issues that you are facing in the relationship. In most cases, men, in particular, do not like to get indulged in relationship talks. Regardless of that, it is important to exchange your wishes and needs with your partner. Communication strategies play a vital role, especially in resolving conflicts. First, you will need to learn about distinguishing between general communication as partners and communication resulting from conflict resolution.

Communicating about each other's wishes, hopes, plans, and ideas forms an important foundation block of a relationship. Those couples who are happy for a long time in their relationships can communicate with each other about their feelings. They do not see the relationship or themselves being threatened by all their expressions. It won't even matter if both of them are negative about their feelings without having an idea about the same. They can develop their gestures, facial expressions, and subtle language throughout their relationship. Fights and quarrels are very normal in a healthy relationship. All that matters are the 'HOW.' Clashes tend to arise whenever you and the other person feel strained by various external stresses. For example, conflicts in the family, problems in raising children, problems in the job, and many others. The partner who feels stressed will communicate with the other person in a more violent or irritated tone.

It is always in your greatest interest to be inventive and proactive about the way you communicate with all those who are closest to you. Creating, nurturing, and maintaining relationships with family, friends, and co-workers, not just our partners, is important for our well-being. Instead of just waiting for others to bring in changes in the relationships, the best and the easiest place for starting is with yourself.

Self-Assessment of a Relationship

Below is a list that offers certain statements that are very common in relationships. Try to check all statements and note any that you think are not true for you. Write them down in a journal.

1. I can get on very well with all the siblings.
2. I have told my partner/children/spouse that I like them within a period of a few weeks or days.
3. I can be friendly with my clients or co-workers.
4. I can get on well with my employees.
5. There is no such person who can make me feel uncomfortable while walking across.
6. I have the habit of positioning relationships at first and results in second.
7. I have successfully destroyed all those relationships that tend to hurt me or injure me.
8. I have tried to communicate will all those people I might have injured, hurt, or disturbed.
9. I do not like or have the habit of gossiping about others.
10. I try to tell the truth all the time, even when I am hurt.

11. I have an effective circle of family or friends who I appreciate and love.
12. I get enough love from everyone around me for feeling appreciated.
13. I always try to stick to my word. Others can rely on me.
14. I always forgive all those people who hurt me.
15. I try my best to clear misunderstandings or miscommunications right after they take place.
16. I do not criticize or judge other people.
17. Nothing is unresolved concerning my past relationships.
18. I live my life completely based on my terms. I do not base my life on the preferences or principles of other people.
19. I am aware of my desires and needs. I make sure others take care of them.
20. I have a lover or supporter.

Problem-Struggles with Household Responsibilities

Most of the partners work at different places or, at times, more than a single job. So, it is very important to divide the responsibilities of the household fairly.

Strategies

- Try to be clear and organized regarding your work or job in your home. You can write down all the roles and decide who is going to do what. It will be better for both partners if you can be clear about the things you do not want to do and want to do. Make sure you figure out the time for all your jobs.
- It is always a good thing to be open to alternatives. If you do not like to take up the job of cleaning your house, you can opt for a cleaning service. In case you focus on being neat, but the other person does not, do you need to compromise? Always try your best for meeting right in the middle. Compromising will lead to future conflicts.

Problem-Money

There are various relationships in which the problems crop up from money. Whether there has been some sort of mistrust because of mismanagement of the finances, or one partner manages finances better than the other, money is capable of easily straining even the rock-solid relationships.

Strategies

- Try to be honest about the present financial scenario. It will be better for you if you do not opt for the topic in tense situations. You can always set a convenient and suitable time when you both can discuss the topic of finance.
- You will need to acknowledge that one of you will always be a saver while the other partner will be a spender. You will need to discuss the positive side of each. Try to learn as much as possible from one another.
- Do not ever hide your financial debts or gains from your partner. If both of you want to join your finances at some point in time, present all the financial documents, along with pay stubs, insurance policies, credit reports, investments, bank statements, and debts.
- If anything goes wrong regarding finances, never try to blame your partner, even if they are at fault. The numbers on your computer screen and the paper pieces are not significant compared to your human bond and connection.
- When you opt for sharing your money, try to bring all your savings under a joint budget. Payout all the monthly bills from that joint budget. Both of you can still put aside some money for spending whenever needed.
- Making decisions about your short-term and long-term goals is very important. It is very normal to have your own goals. However, you should not also underestimate your family goals.
- It is a natural thing when one partner takes more financial responsibilities than the other. In such cases, never try to undermine your partner if you are the one who takes more responsibility.

Problem-Not Keeping the Relationship on the Priority List

If you are willing to maintain the relationship and want to keep it healthy, prioritizing is very important. Try to understand its importance. Try to cherish your relationship and nourish the same. This way, you can stand out with your partner in the relationship in the test of time.

Strategies

- Start doing all those things that you used to do during the initial days of the relationship. It is said that the starting days of a relationship are always the most soothing ones. Give compliments to each other, appreciate each other, communicate with each other throughout the day, and showcase genuine interest in one another.
- Try to take out some time from the busy schedule and go on a date. Try to plan the date with the level of consideration, just like you both were trying to win over each other during the initial days.
- Always keep in mind that respect is a very important component of a healthy relationship. In case you cannot appreciate someone much, learn to do that. When your partner tries to do something that genuinely makes you smile or happy, do not hesitate to show gratitude by simply saying thank you. Just let your partner understand what matters to you and him/her.

Problem-Conflicts

Occasional fights and conflicts are very natural and are more or less part of our lives. But in case you and your partner keep arguing all the time, the time has come to break the cycle. You both need to get freed from such a poisonous routine. In place of just igniting your anger, try to look closely into the underlying problems. Try to find out how you can solve the problem without any risk of hostility.

Solution

- Both of you will need to argue in a useful and civil manner. It can help in suppressing the fire of conflict.
- You will need to realize that you are not the victim. It is perfectly your choice for reacting the way you do. Try to be honest with yourself, along with your partner, regarding how you truly feel.
- Once you are in the center of a heated argument, try to pay attention to how you phrase things along with the voice tone. Will you be feeling okay if your partner also spoke to you in the same way, in the same tone? You will need to put kindness and love first. Never forget that the individual you are arguing with is also the person you have chosen to be your life partner. Do you find

the conflict of more worth than your relationship? Try to respect the relationship along with your partner, even while arguing. If you want to prove a point, just stay calm and explain yourself to your partner with a soothing tone and not something violent.

- If you keep on responding with a similar kind of approach that already invited unhappiness and pain in your life, it will be foolish of you if you expect something different. For instance, if you have the habit of stopping your partner in the middle while he/she talks just because you are willing to defend yourself, stop doing that for some time. You will feel amazed and shocked after seeing how much a tempo change can affect your argument tone.
- Do not hesitate to apologize to your partner when you realize that you are the wrong one. It is a great way in which you can show your partner that you respect their values much ahead of being right. Just try this and see the results.
- You can never manage or control the behavior of someone else. You need to remember that the only person whom you can control is yourself. So, when you try to shift your focus from your partner's behavior and concentrate on yours, you will find it easier to resolve any conflict.

Problem-Trust

Trust is very important as far as a healthy relationship is concerned. Are you concentrating on all those things that might make your trust in your romantic partner fade away? Are you having certain issues that are not resolved yet and are making it tough for you to trust your partner? If that is the case, you will need to work on the same as soon as possible. Whenever trust issues crop up in a relationship, the chances are high that it will weaken the relationship's foundation if not taken care of properly.

Strategies

You can develop trust in your partner and vice versa if both of you try to consider the mentioned pointers.

- Try to be punctual.
- Try not to be inconsistent.
- Try being fair, even while arguing.
- Never fail at doing all that you have promised.

- Stop yourself from lying, no matter what the situation is.
- Call up when you have that you will.
- Try being sensitive to the feelings of your partner. You might still disagree with your partner but do not undermine his/her feelings.
- Let your partner know whenever you will be reaching home late.
- Try to carry your weight. Fulfill all your responsibilities and promises.
- Always keep yourself away from old wounds.
- Try not to say those things that you can never take back.
- Prevent yourself from being jealous without any need.
- Have respect for the boundaries of your partner.
- Try to be realistic. When you just think that your romantic partner will be able to meet all your needs and wants, while you expect them to understand everything without expressing what you need, it can be treated as a fantasy from a Hollywood movie. Just ask your partner for all that you need and do not just expect them to read your mind.

You are always required to be all ready for making the relationship work from all positive sides. Try to look into those things that need to be done for keeping up the healthy state of the relationship. Do not just conclude that you cannot maintain a loving and peaceful relationship with your partner until and unless you give a look over the conflicts. Make sure you address them all. If you fail to attend to all the active issues in your relationship, your relationship will be marred by all of these problems.

CHAPTER 7: ACCEPTING YOURSELF AND YOUR PARTNER

In any relationship, we need to accept our partners the way they are; no one is perfect, and an important thing to remember is that perfection is a myth. No one in this world is perfect, and everyone has flaws. If you come into your relationship thinking that your partner is perfect and that you won't have any issues, then this is creating very unrealistic expectations. It is because they did not realize that chasing perfection does not get you anywhere. Instead of trying to make everything perfect, accept your partner how they are and love them unconditionally.

When we decide to share our life with someone else, we've already taken the time to get to know them, and we take the time to understand who they are and what they're about when we take the step to join our lives with them forever, we have told them that we accept them for who they are Is after you have gotten in a relationship you find that this is not true anymore than your relationship needs work a relationship cannot work if you do not accept your partner for who they are By that same logic by that same logic your partner and yourself will have bed communication and find that you are unable to communicate as efficiently as you'd like to because you feel that your partner does not understand you which can lead to feelings of neglect.

Remember that you do not want your partner to have unrealistic expectations of you, so you should not have unrealistic expectations for him/her either. If you want your relationship to work, then you will need to understand the importance of being able to make sure that you are thinking realistically.

When you become frustrated with your partner, you need to pull back and recognize what it is you are thinking. Is what you are thinking something that your partner needs to change, or is it something that you've built up in your mind because you have unrealistic expectations about what they should be or what you want them to be? Is it something you need to change with your thought process, or is it something that genuinely needs to be changed in your partner? Another question that you should ask yourself is, why is it your partner's job to live up to unrealistic expectations? On the opposite side to this, why is it your job to live up to your partner's unrealistic expectations? You need to realize that having the right expectations of yourself, your partner, and your relationship are the best ways that you are going to be able to make this relationship work.

Flexibility is another thing that is going to help you appreciate your partner and make sure that you are accepting him/her the way he/she is. It is very easy to think of the world as just black or just white and think that this is wrong, or this is right, and there is no in-between, but that's not realistic. Things do not have to be one way or the other. Instead of labeling your way as the right way or your partner's way as the right way, remember that you need to compromise and understand how things are.

Negative thinking is much easier for some people than positive thinking because being negative does not require half as much effort as being positive. When a person is being negative and thinking negatively, it is very self-imposed and self-centered behavior. When we think negatively, we are not accepting our partner for who he/she is, and instead, we see the negative in him/her because we are focusing on being negative ourselves. Being positive instead of focusing on why your partner is the way that he/she is will cause you to be able to focus on what's amazing about him/her and why you like him/her in the first place. This, in turn, will lead you to accept him/her for who he/she is, and this will lead to you appreciating him/her for who he/she is as well. Just as you need the love of your partner to make you happy and whole, your partner needs your love to make him/her happy and whole as well. He/she needs you to be here for him/her as well.

Another helpful hint to appreciating your partner is to force yourself to see things in a different light and put the focus on you. What we mean by this is that you should ask yourself how you would feel if your partner was judging you the way that you are judging him/her. Another question you should ask is that if he/she did not accept you the way that you are not accepting him/her, how would you feel if you thought your partner did not understand you or love you the way that you needed to be loved and respected? Keeping this in mind, you'll be much more flexible, and you'll be able to understand why you should not treat your partner this way.

You should also strive to remember that the past is gone, and there is nothing you can do about it. You can make up for the past. That part is possible, and we're not saying that it is not. What we're saying is whatever happened in the past, you can't go back in time and make it so that did not happen. There are no do-overs or a reset button on the things you do because life is not a video game. It is here and now, and you need to learn that if you make a mistake, you can't undo it, but you can fix it and move on from it. You just need to remember that whatever has happened has already happened, and there's nothing you can do to change that. We all make mistakes, so instead of focusing on the past, try living in the present and give your partner the gift of understanding that.

If you are always comparing things to how they were before or you are always comparing things to the past and bringing up past arguments along with things that can't be changed, the only thing that you are doing is hindering your acceptance of your partner and your acceptance of each other. If this continues over time, it could end up destroying your relationship because you are not focusing on the future the way that you need to be. The biggest reason that this is an issue that can be so damaging is because when you are doing this, it brings resentment and past pain to the relationship. This, in turn, brings hurt into the relationship, along with fighting and harsh words. To avoid this, you should focus on the present and what you can do in the present to change things to make them better for your partner and yourself.

When we judge others, it is often a result of our criticisms that we've had to endure ourselves, but we should not put pressure on ourselves to do things a certain way, and we should not put pressure on our partner to do things that way either. Letting what others have said to you or done to you can affect you and your thought process and the way you treat others, including your partner. This is why people say your past shapes who you are. If you were abused when you were younger or had bad relationships, you can unintentionally drag it into your future relationships even though you do not mean to. The way to get past this is to understand that is what you've got this issue in the first place and then work on trying to change. In the long run, this will ensure that your heart and spirit are happier and more fulfilled. It will cause your treatment of your partner to get better and make sure that your partner's spirit and heart are happier too.

When you put unnecessary pressure on your partner, the only thing you are doing is pushing him/her away. Now every relationship has pressure, and every relationship has areas where your partner will be under pressure but what we're saying is instead of judging yourself and judging others, understand that everyone has limitations. You can't put too much pressure on someone because he/she will crack. It may not happen right away, especially if your partner is strong, but eventually, even the strongest person can break if you keep pushing him/her too hard. If you cause your partner to crack, then your relationship will falter immediately because he/she is going to feel resentment towards you for doing so. When you are happy and fulfilled as an individual, you will be less critical and rude to your partner.

CHAPTER 8: WHY ARE RELATIONSHIPS COMPLEX?

Having a partnership to last will often feel like a very difficult mission because it is very complex. Most of us can develop a relationship that lasts a lifetime, while others just don't manage to make things happen, despite being initially comfortable with each other.

The Life Cycle of a Relationship

Relationships tend to go through five levels-some are more satisfying than others. So, if you and your partner can work together with each stage as they arrive, the incentives will be combined with the development and a stronger relationship. However, get caught in one of these stages, and you and your better half could simply wind up attempting to give up.

Falling in Love

Also called the "fixation period." It is the most glamorized period of the cycle of marriage. It's something that happens in the movies, and it's something that any of us care about!

Our human nature causes us to fall in love with each other. According to Dr. Susan Campbell, our brains emit a bunch of hormones designed to make us feel attractive. Oxytocin, serotonin, and phenylethylamine (a stimulant of the nervous system, and a very hard word to pronounce) form a concoction that renders you as happy as heaven on fatty love.

A road trip just helps you to see the differences between you and your partner, as well as the qualities that make him/her a good person. All this will allow you to see his/her weaknesses and shortcomings.

This doesn't always have to be a bad thing; we all have faults and characteristics that we'd prefer to keep to ourselves until we're more confident. Unless it wasn't for infatuation, we'd all be single!

After a time of growing up, our passion deepens and becomes relaxed with each other. Finally, we have a closer connection with our partner; we feel protected and treasured. A lot of people misinterpret that as the highest degree of affection we should have gotten, but they'd be mistaken.

Infatuated drug-love wears off-Campbell extends this wear-off from two months to two years depending on the pair. Deepened passion continues a time after that until the 3–4-year point of a relationship. Yet instead we're going to reach the risk zone.

The Reality Check

This is better known as "the love hangover" or "the disillusionment period." According to Dr. Campbell, an incredibly large number of marriages are taking place at this time. At this point, we begin to reflect on our weaknesses and shortcomings, rather than on the ways we are. The passion we have can be replaced by frustration and anger.

We can continue to get irritated with the little stuff more often than not. We will feel less cared about or loved than we used to do. Before this point, it was all right (though difficult to be parted) to let each other concentrate on work tasks-now, choosing work over each other feels like negligence.

At this point, we sometimes make the error of attempting to "transform" our partners by punishment: disagreement, violent conduct, and emotional isolation, the list goes on.

How can you work your way through this tough patch successfully? This stage is a time to reflect on your interactions-most importantly on the ability to settle disputes Campbell's tips for getting through this point include:

- Acknowledging and appreciating your similarities.
- Sharing control and knowing dominance won't get you what you want.
- Recognizing that peace without conflict doesn't happen.
- Embracing life because it is now time to remind yourself of your own personal. Shortcomings and failures, and to reflect on how your spouse makes up for them. Know what makes a team of you!

If you can't settle your differences successfully at this point, you can find yourself coming back to it regularly in your relationship. Some people have been trapped in this stage for years-never hitting the next point-until they stopped calling.

Stability

You've worked out how to compromise with-and, not a fight-your friend. Congratulations, you've made a hell of a past relationship, and passion is back! Phase one's older, smarter brother is the stabilization stage. At this point, you've embraced each other for who you are, and you don't want to change them anymore (you've never been able to do that anyway).

You have strong boundaries for each other at this point, as well as reciprocal respect. This love is true; it lasts. Today, with more faith than ever before, you can tell that you love each other completely for who you are.

Even in moments of disagreement or immaturity, it is understood that hurtful conduct is not due to either of you being cruel or uncaring. Yes, at times, you could struggle and have your differences. Yet this doesn't preclude you from maintaining a close bond with them.

However, at this point, some couples end their relationships. Stability can make certain people feel nervous or bored. Although it's normal to skip the thrilling infatuation of stage 1, some people are beginning to wonder if they can get that back with a new boyfriend. It may be the ignition that would set off an extramarital affair. Our advice, huh? Weigh what you've got to earn against what you've got to lose. Though falling in love can be fun and thrilling, it doesn't last forever.

Commitment

At the point when you're intending to get hitched, this is the stage you're going to need to be in before you pose an inquiry. Couples now understand that while they needn't bother with one another (speedy updates that people will truly exist all alone), they need to be with one another, deficiencies or not.

Some people don't skip stage one; the only other way to get back to that is to meet someone new to marry, so they don't want anything else except their partner. Commitment is a real symbol of long-lasting devotion.

Happiness

In the happiness point, people step past the inner workings of their partnership-they've got all packed up by now-and out into the world around them. Such couples prefer to collaborate on projects together. To certain couples, it means launching a company or a charity together. For some, this stage involves working together to grow up and sustain a family. Among these purposes, this period is most sometimes referred to as the period of co-creation.

Couples seem to spend several years at this point. Yet it's always important to note to carry on sustaining your relationship while spending this time and energy in their new passions!

Please note, these steps are not sequential, so happiness is not always an end goal. Numerous individuals experience these periods a few times in their relationships, months or years, one after another.

This is crucial to have the option to perceive the phase you and your partner are in, so you can settle on more advantageous choices on whether to improve your relationship, instead of making somebody stage debilitate or fall apart.

CONCLUSION

Romantic relationships require hard work; we all know it well. Like cars, they need some regular maintenance to maintain their performance. If a problem happens, it should be fixed immediately to avoid further complications.

We can often do some essential maintenance and repair ourselves. Other times, we have to rely on a specialist to look and to give us a hand, given our efforts.

It is interesting that we take such steps easily and quickly to repair or prevent further damage to our vehicles. But we often avoid acting in our relationships until the situation gets much severe.

Unfortunately, many couples have tried couple therapy when considerable damage has been done already. Maladaptive relationship patterns have become strong, the emotional bonds between partners have severely weakened, and the unresolved past conflicts cause a high level of resentment. The list can continue.

Research supports couples' therapy as an effective way to strengthen their partnership. While there are few reasons to support therapy, many marriage therapy activities help people develop their communication skills, minimize disruptive conduct habits, and enhance their capabilities to be emotionally receptive and attentive to their partners.

If you consider counseling people but don't know if your effort would be worth it, you are not alone. Perhaps you learned about a friend's lack of success or attempted it yourself without much profit.

Good results are more likely when couples who undergo therapy are eager to learn practical skills and become both more self-aware and emotionally insecure. Only fundamental communication skills, such as "feeling" words, are required. Most people find it challenging to distinguish between emotions and thoughts. This ability can also be acquired and enhanced during the therapy process.

A second most important feature of successful couples is their ability to avoid treating each other as a foe, but rather as a member of the team, collaborating to enhance mutual happiness, seeing you as "in the same team" increases collaboration and the ability of each person to be emotionally sensitive.

Thirdly, the partner's ability to feel empathy is essential. Every person must have compassion for the feelings of insecurity of others and past emotional traumas.

Finally, the willingness of each person to play their part in the problems and to make a positive change is a prerequisite for successful couples' work. Most people undergo relationship therapy with a list of the other person's grievances and want to see a therapist confirm the grievances and then alter the other person's actions. Although complaints are often valid, nothing can be resolved unless both people are ready to change some element of their conduct.

I hope that the first part of the ideas I shared will strengthen your relationship with your partner. Expect that there are stormy days in your relationship but facing them together is a sure way to overcome the difficulties. It is significant to have an open line of communication to be able to resolve whatever problems you may encounter in your relationship.

Keep the passion alive and sizzling because it brings pleasure and happiness. Cultivate the relationship with love, trust, and commitment. It will steer you away from temptations, heartaches, and tears. Make it a habit to rekindle your passion every day by showing how much you mean to each other.

Remember that it always takes two people to build a relationship and two people to make it lasts. It's all in your hands.

INTRODUCTION OVERCOME INSECURITY IN LOVE

Relationships have heaven's feel and look; however, they can become hell for your life. It does not indicate the arrangement is false, just because there are things that need to be resolved to recover and intensify the passion. Such problems have different explanations for doing so. If we're with somebody we love and who loves us, we generally feel protected, recognized, and acknowledged by whom we truly like we are with. Consequently, a variety of things may happen.

We typically feel comfortable enough to relax completely, unwittingly facilitating the appearance of certain facets of ourselves. Aspects that are not inherently "negative" but where we realize others feel challenging, and we generally cover or regulate them.

We may begin to unintentionally replay our past experiences in intimate circumstances, particularly those from our infancy. If someone feels too unloved by his parents, then as an adult, he or she could search for someone to love him. The problem could get worse if, much like his parents, any girlfriend he falls in love with starts moving away from him. He will unintentionally replay his memory, as that's what he feels more familiar with-obviously, "being relaxed" feels what we're seeking, isn't it?

Similarly, we can unintentionally impose our desires on our spouse-for example, when we want to do so much for them, often to the point that we are forced away when in reality it's us that need the support! Consider the example of a housewife who wants to make things easy for her husband by maintaining the house immaculate, preparing nutritious meals, washing, and ironing, and functioning full time. Eventually, her husband begins to feel suffocated and spends less and less time in the house. The woman will get panicky and doesn't grasp what is wrong with her. What she struggles to understand is that she is focusing all her time and money on her friend and little on herself. She is the one who wants affection and attention, something that may never have been felt. Nevertheless, if she goes on with her actions, her friendship will turn acidic and bitter.

Unconsciously, we may demand our spouse to satisfy all of our needs! We give up making our own choices, submit to whatever our spouse wishes, and often get angry with their choices. We may do so because it helps our companion feel "important" or because it will not make them irritable. This may also be that we're afraid to make the "wrong" choice, don't know what we want, or simply feel confused. In reality, as you are prohibited from having trust in your abilities to make good choices, such a concern occurs. You also relinquish the obligation to your mate.

Relationships can sometimes cause major worries. If you start challenging your spouse and avoid trusting him or her, your spouse will feel confused and afraid and pushed apart.

Remember that many of these problems emerge unintentionally and have little to do with whether or how much we enjoy our mate or how much they value us; such are the checks and obstacles that sometimes occur in reaction to the instinctive desire toward greater intimacy. If you refuse to approach these things rationally, your world transforms into chaos. This is where the problem is critical. How much do we love our partner? How important to us is the relationship? How much do we expect our spouse to remain in our lives? Is it enough to inspire us to address these problems-issues that sometimes allow us to deal with difficult facets of ourselves? If they weren't uncomfortable or intense, they would have tried to solve them earlier.

Intimate relationships are a mirror that represents the best and worst of us all. They can inflame or soothe our burdens. They might sound like sorcery when they're perfect. Sometimes though they are exactly correct, fear will rob the magic and break the bond between two entities that belong together. All partnerships call for trust, tenderness, persistence, and weakness. Individuals with anxiety also have these by the truckload and can lend the partnership kindly. The trouble is that, often, fear will erode them almost as easily.

This second part of the book will also help you light your love life and keep your heart and mind full of love, peace, security, and value. Take your time to read it, take notes as you read each page, and treat it as a practical guide.

CHAPTER 9: CONFLICT BETWEEN COUPLES

Unsurprisingly, many married couples suffer quite similar challenges, the majority of which are resolvable, avoidable, or repairable.

1. **Sexual difference:** While some may find it awkward to admit it, the physical connection is necessary for long-lasting partnerships. As a result, sexual incompatibility and libido loss are common problems for married couples.
2. **Beliefs and values:** There will always be disagreements in a marriage, which is perfectly normal. It is beneficial to engage in debates and conversations about a variety of subjects. Unfortunately, some distinctions are simply too great to ignore. These are frequently referred to as an individual's beliefs or values. These are also frequently rejected or neglected during the early stages of a relationship, but they can develop into severe marital problems over time.
3. **Life stages:** While this subject is frequently disregarded in discussions about relationships, the issue of life stages is pervasive, particularly in our modern, fast-paced culture. Occasionally, the basis of marital conflict is a partner's desire for something else in life. These difficulties are especially prevalent in partnerships between couples with a substantial age difference.
4. **Stress:** This one occurs at least once in almost every marriage. Stress can be triggered by a variety of factors, including familial, mental health, or financial concerns. How this stress is managed can have a big impact on the importance of this issue in a marriage.

Issues That Put Even Happy Marriages at Risk

Issues are not exclusive to people in bad marriages; they can also bother even the healthiest couples. The distinction between successful and terrible marriages, however, is in how these issues are addressed and how much each partner permits the issue to escalate before resolving it. Even in a good marriage, one issue that frequently rears its ugly head is overstepping boundaries.

According to studies, once a couple marries, it is not rare for one of the spouses to switch partners. This could be anything from their values to their appearance-the spouse tries to modify their spouse.

These attempts can create friction between the relationship, which can become destructive if left unresolved. Infidelity can also manifest itself emotionally in a loving marriage. Thus, even if there is no physical adultery, emotional adultery can occur when two people drift apart and develop relationships with persons outside the marriage.

It's sometimes comforting to know that even individuals in successful marriages can encounter difficulties. This can help put your relationship concerns into context and allow you to be a bit kinder to yourself.

Relationship Mistakes

Everybody makes mistakes in relationships, even those that last a long time. Expecting that neither you nor your partner will ever make a relationship error is unreasonable. Maintaining an unreasonable standard can result in undue pressure being placed on a relationship, which can result in different challenges.

The severity of errors varies. Some can be fixed with time and dialogue, while others are difficult to recover from. Taking your mate for granted is a typical relationship error. As a relationship matures and deepens, it's natural to fall into a new life routine.

That is all well and good. However, partners can get overly comfortable, to the point that they begin to take their significant other for granted. Another error that some people make as relationships progress is to remove their privacy boundaries.

At first, a deep relationship is built through protecting each other's best-kept secrets and developing a reputation as a trustworthy source of information for your spouse. However, if these secrets are gradually revealed to close friends and family, they might introduce additional concerns of trust and anxiety into the relationship.

Money Conflicts

As a relationship develops, your lives become increasingly entwined. This is a wonderful thing since it connects each spouse into the lives of the other, allowing for the sharing of additional memories. These memories include vacations, pets, automobile purchases, and even homeownership. All these milestones are critical and vital for a relationship, but they also come with financial concerns.

Occasionally, conflicts can occur as a result of a partner's excessive spending habits. You may get uncomfortable with their expenditures on stuff such as clothing, shoes, and other non-essential stuff. It is critical to gain a deeper understanding of one another and reach a point of agreement to express why you feel one way and your partner feels another.

Another difficulty that can arise in a money-related relationship is the question of saving money. You may have divergent views on how much money you should save each week, which might result in arguments on how to save money. Again, it is critical to discuss these problems to acquire a better understanding of how your partner thinks and why they feel differently about saving than you do. You will then be able to establish mutually beneficial savings goals that will hopefully suit the objectives of both parties.

Defending One's Point of View Determinately

In any relationship, it is critical to stand up for what you believe in. If you abandon your principles and convictions to keep your partner happy and avoid conflict, you will eventually find yourself unhappy and apprehensive about the relationship.

Someone's perspective and opinions are a significant element of what makes each of us unique. It's also quite possible that this is one of the primary reasons your spouse fell for you in the first place. As a result, it's critical to understand how to defend oneself without coming across as defensive to maintain your points of view intact.

When expressing your viewpoint on a subject, ensure that you have conducted sufficient study. When you offer an idea, there will always be some who concur, but there will also always be those who disagree.

Additionally, ensure that you are open to constructive criticism. It is one thing to express verbal gratitude. However, by demonstrating that you are absorbing information, you demonstrate to your partner that you are willing to listen and learn and that they should be as well. Possessing a strong point of view also necessitates a great deal of patience. It's possible that your partner initially does not understand, and that's fine. Be prepared to stick to your guns, and they will eventually understand how critical that specific subject is to you.

Issues That Contribute to a Divorce in Crisis

Avoid Them at All Costs. "Crisis" is a large term that should only be used when essential! As a result, it is critical to address these possible concerns before they escalate into a crisis that could result in divorce.

1. **Libido loss:** It's pointless to pretend that sex isn't a significant element of any relationship. If you allow it, your sex life in marriage can deteriorate with time. As a result, it is critical to have a good sexual relationship with your spouse. Communicate your preferences and dissatisfactions. Continue to instill the desire in your partner through your acts and words.
2. **Emotional or physical infidelity:** Both emotional and physical infidelity are difficult to overcome if left unresolved. Physically cheating on someone is a difficult step to overcome in some situations, and it might result in divorce in others. Additionally, knowing that your partner has cheated on you emotionally or physically might result in increased levels of tension and worry.
3. **Financial disagreements:** Another difficulty that can emerge throughout the marriage is financial disagreements. These might stem from a variety of factors, including how money is spent or saved. These conflicts may begin modest at first, but if not addressed thoroughly, they can escalate into additional anger.

Two Couple's Secret Sexual Issues

Finally, disagreements between spouses over sexual concerns boil down to two major concerns. These two issues are more prevalent than you might believe, and how you resolve them as a couple is critical to the relationship's continued growth and prosperity.

There is frequently one partner who is dissatisfied with the amount of sex in the relationship, to begin with. This could be a partner who wishes they had more sex together or a spouse who wishes they made love less frequently. Without being addressed, this irritation may breed additional animosity over time.

This can become a problem that spreads to other areas of the relationship, so it's critical to halt the spread of these difficulties by early communication. It will enable partners to gain a deeper understanding of one another before moving forward with the relationship. This leads us to our second point, communication. Couples frequently struggle to communicate what they appreciate and dislike in the bedroom.

This can occasionally result in a less pleasurable and intimate bedroom experience, impeding the entire relationship's advancement.

Couple's Common Concerns and Issues

1. How Do I Know They're the One

It can be tough to determine whether someone is "the one" for you at times. Regrettably, some friends make it appear so clear with their relationship that it causes you to doubt your sentiments. Always keep in mind that everyone's emotions are unique, and your relationship cannot be compared to another. As a result, determining whether someone is the one is difficult. However, if you like spending time with your partner and envision a future together, this is typically a positive indicator.

2. I Am Not Yet Prepared to Marry but My Partner Is

This is pretty frequent and makes a lot of sense when you think about it. How likely are you and your partner to be in the same emotional place at the same time? If your spouse is a good match for you, they will respect your viewpoint and patiently wait for you to mature in your own time.

3. I Have the Impression That My Partner Does Not Trust Me

This can be a challenging situation and must be handled cautiously. To begin, it's worthwhile to discuss this emotion with your partner, explaining why you're feeling this way. This enables your spouse to address why they may lack faith in you or why they are unwilling to alter their conduct. It will serve as a beginning point for adjusting your relationship as necessary.

Ways of Resolving Conflicts in Marriage

Conflict is an unavoidable component of nearly all relationships. Additionally, it can be a major source of stress. As a result, it is critical to resolving most confrontations. This may seem self-evident, but many people hide their anger or simply "go along to get along." Some believe that by resolving a disagreement, they are actually creating one and hence prefer to remain silent while angered. Regrettably, this is not a sustainable long-term plan. Unresolved disagreement in a relationship can breed resentment and further unresolved conflict. Even more concerning, a persistent dispute can have a detrimental effect on one's health and longevity.

Regrettably, overcoming disagreements can also be challenging. When handled correctly, attempts at mediation can exacerbate the issue. For instance, John Gottman and his colleagues investigated how couples fight and discovered that they could predict which couples will divorce based on their conflict resolution skills or lack thereof.

Couples who are continuously attacking their partner's character or withdrawing during disagreements, rather than resolving a dispute in a proactive, polite manner, should be on their guard.

For individuals who were not born into a home where excellent conflict resolution skills were demonstrated regularly (and, let's face it, how many of us were?), here are some principles for simplifying and de-stressing dispute resolution.

Connect with Your Emotions

A critical component of conflict resolution includes simply understanding how and why you feel the way you do. While it may appear that your feelings should be self-evident, this is not always the case. At times, you may feel angry or bitter for no apparent reason. In other instances, you may feel as though the other person is not doing what they "should," but you are unsure of what you want from them or whether your request is even realistic.

Journaling can be an excellent approach to connect with your own emotions, thoughts, and expectations to transmit them more effectively to the other person.

Occasionally, this process brings up some quite serious concerns, for which counseling may be beneficial.

Develop Your Listening Ability

When it comes to effective dispute resolution, listening skills are at least as crucial as speaking skills. It is critical to grasp the other person's perspective in addition to our own if we are to reach an agreement.

Indeed, simply assisting the other person in feeling heard and understood can frequently go a long way toward resolving a problem. Additionally, effective listening enables you to bridge the divide between the two of you, identify the source of the disconnect, and so forth.

Unfortunately, active listening is a skill that not everyone possesses, and it is common for people to believe they are listening while crafting their next reaction, thinking to themselves how wrong the other person is, or engaging in other activities unrelated to attempting to grasp the other person's perspective. Additionally, it is common to be so defensive and ensconced in your perspective that you are unable to hear the other person.

Develop Assertive Communication Skills

Communicating your feelings and needs openly is also critical in resolving conflicts. As you are surely aware, saying the incorrect thing can exacerbate a quarrel. What's critical to remember is to express yourself clearly and assertively, without being confrontational or putting the other person on the defensive.

One effective method for resolving conflict is to express yourself in terms of how you feel, rather than what you believe the other person is doing incorrectly, by utilizing "I feel" phrases.

Look for a Resolution

Once you've gained an understanding of the other person's perspective and they've gained an understanding of yours, it's time to resolve the conflict-a solution that both parties can live with. Occasionally, a simple and obvious solution emerges when both parties grasp the other's perspective. When a quarrel is the result of misunderstanding or a lack of understanding of the other's perspective, a simple apology can work wonders, and an open discussion can bring people together.

In other instances, a bit more effort is required. When two people disagree on a topic, you have a few options. Occasionally, you may agree to disagree, occasionally, you may reach a compromise or a middle ground, and occasionally, the person who feels more strongly about an issue may get their way with the understanding that they will concede the next time. The critical point is to get an understanding and attempt to resolve issues in a manner that is respectful of all parties concerned.

Recognize When It Isn't Working

Due to the toll that ongoing disagreement may exact on an individual, it is often prudent to maintain some distance in a relationship or to cut ties completely.

Simple conflict resolution tactics will only go you so far in times of abuse, and personal safety must take precedence.

On the other side, when dealing with challenging family members, putting a few limits and respecting the other person's limits in the relationship can bring about some calm. In unsupportive friendships or those marked by chronic conflict, letting go can be a significant source of stress alleviation. Only you can determine whether a relationship can be improved or if it should be terminated.

CHAPTER 10: OVERCOMING RELATIONSHIP INSECURITY

The biggest step towards overcoming your insecurities in a relationship is first improving the capacity to discern your insecurities. It's so very easy to rationalize away your insecurities. for instance, if you tend to follow your partner around simply because you can't stand being alone, you might decide to call it "love," when it is an obsession and an indication of deep-seated insecurities. These are some important tips for ridding yourself of insecurities:

Quit Comparing Yourself to Others

Most insecure people have a negative habit of wanting to rate themselves against their partner's exes. They try to find out various things about their partner's exes; what did they achieve? Were they beautiful or handsome? What schools did they go to? Were they successful in their careers? All of this information is carefully analyzed, and the insecure person holds onto hope that they are better than the exes, but when that is not the case, it gives them grief. The first step in overcoming insecurities in relationships is to stop comparing yourself with other people regardless of what role they play in your partner's life. What matters is that your partner has you at present.

Embrace Your Quirkiness

Human beings are social animals. We want to fit in and look like the rest, but for some strange reason, some people don't have an easy time fitting in with the rest. What must they do? Should they force themselves to become what they are not? Certainly not! Such people ought to embrace their quirky traits wholeheartedly. When you become self-confident and start to express yourself fully, others who are like you, who admire what you are, will be drawn to you. Sadly, people who stand out tend to harbor insecurities that ultimately ruin their relationships.

Create Some Boundaries

Did you know that predators have an innate capability to sense the weak ones? If you have insecurities, you pretty much qualify as a weak person; maybe you'll hate the thought of being abandoned by your partner and start letting them do as they please. This can result in your partner taking advantage of you, abusing you, shredding to bits any ounce of self-esteem that was left. If you want to overcome your insecurities, you must learn to create some boundaries and enforce your rules if your partner oversteps them. one of the most common ways that people are abused in relationships is on resources. The predator might dip their hands into the savings of their insecure partner and waste them away. Create boundaries to ensure that you are treated with respect, and this will allow your subconscious mind to promote your full recovery into emotional stability and high self-esteem.

Build Your Self-Confidence

One undeniable fact is that nothing significant can be accomplished when self-confidence is lacking. But the funny thing is that self-confidence is not an inborn trait but rather a skill that one can learn and embolden with more practice. Every leader you can think of is self-confident. that is not mean they are arrogant, but rather, they consider themselves valuable, and they are ready and willing to fight for what they want. If you would want to overcome your insecurities, you should first build your self-confidence so that you may have the courage to speak up and say what you want for yourself.

Start Trusting Again

There's a reason someone shows insecurities in a relationship; usually, something happened to them. Maybe one or both of their parents abandoned them when they were little and needy. Maybe they were abused. You never know what happened. and these experiences wiped out their ability to trust anybody else, and that's why they cannot believe whatever their partner says, always needing affirmations, etc. but to kick away insecurities, one must learn to trust people again. of course, not everyone can be trusted, but you must be willing to depend on people to cure yourself of insecurities.

Go to the Root Cause

Fighting away your insecurities is not a walk in the park. You have to rise above your ego and admit to yourself that you have a deep-seated cause of your insecurities. When you admit to yourself that you have a problem, it becomes a lot easier to overcome this problem. Usually, the root cause of insecurities is a nasty experience, particularly during one's childhood.

By acknowledging the fact that you are struggling with an unresolved traumatic experience and then confronting this trauma, you will be in a position to restore your emotional stability, increase your confidence, and get rid of your harmful negative beliefs.

Stop Taking Things Personally

Most insecure people have a huge weakness of always thinking that they are targeted personally. They have a twisted perception of reality, and as a result, they are hurt by things that don't hurt "normal" people. To stop taking things personally, you have to increase your mental toughness and have a big heart. Don't go looking for evidence that the world is out to get you, but instead, focus on the positive side of things. If your partner makes a statement, don't dwell on the negative connotation (if there's any), but try to perceive the message in a positive light. For instance, if you prepare food and your partner remarks that the salt was extra, don't take it that your partner thinks less of you as a cook, but that they don't particularly appreciate excess salt.

Get a Hobby

So many people get depressed and insecure in relationships because they have gotten a lot of time to be idle. If you do nothing but sit around in front of a TV with a remote in one hand and the other hand free to extend into a box of doughnuts, you'll soon balloon into a large person, develop a negative self-image, and start being insecure. But when you are using your time constructively, you will have less time to think about your inadequacies. Fill out your free time with indulgence in your favorite hobbies.

Create Goals

When you have a goal, you are deciding to focus on something bigger than you, and in most cases, you are inviting various people to cooperate with you. Great goals will allow you to channel your mental resources into the activities that matter, and you will be less likely to think about your asymmetrical face, terrible figure, anxiety, and whatever else that might make you think less of yourself. More often than not, goals can be monetized, and not to say that the secret of happiness is money, but then you are in a position to create a healthier life.

Improve Your Social Circle

for some reason, most people who are insecure in relationships tend not to have any friends. It almost seems like their partner is where life begins and ends. That's a pitiful way of living. Being clingy won't make your partner love you more; on the contrary, it will make them tired of you, and they may resent you. Put some distance between yourself and your partner by creating awesome relationships with other people, i.e., friends. When you need to socialize, you can always go out to these people, and you will come back feeling revitalized. But then ensure you are not so into friends that you forget about your partner.

CHAPTER 11: FEAR OF ABANDONMENT IN A RELATIONSHIP

The first step in living with someone is to quench their fear of abandonment. Saying it is far easier than doing it. This has to be done, though. Within yourself and your relationships, you have to build up your trust. You must know that you are caring and worthy of love. You must understand. You must learn how to realize, by enhancing your self-esteem, that you deserve love and to find someone deserving of your affection. Perhaps you can't do it all on your own. For better assistance, you can hire licensed therapists for this very subject online. Virtual counseling is completely professional and private but provides full therapy from your own home.

It's a difficult next step. You must have faith. It is a humble fight for certain people, in particular, if they have lost their past faith in love. Yet, a new effort is worth any new person in our lives. We can't punish them for mistakes made by someone else. Enable all attempts to keep them in your life instead of living each day waiting for them to leave you. This does not mean that you should tolerate violent or unpleasant acts. However, do not set your connection up for failure before it had the chance to start. The use of licensed practitioners, as described above, is an ideal way to deal with these issues.

I Am Doomed

No! Anybody can change at any given moment. This can happen without professional assistance and advice, but it is not easy, which means that assistance from a professional is recommended.

If you let go of the anxiety, you will feel like you have lifted a heavyweight from your shoulders, and you will be finding those relationships you want to live. You'll believe you deserve that love from the bottom of your heart and can work to build that relationship instead of sabotaging it with fear.

Know that you have people who love you and care for you. Fear can be weakening, but it can be an enjoyable feeling and worth overcoming a weakening fear in the long run.

Identify and correct issues in abandonment before you are seriously involved. Before you continue, please ask yourself, "Do I have problems with abandonment?" You will continue in a loop of choosing the wrong partners, which will ultimately result in an unhappy marriage unless you accept your deep feelings and acknowledge them. It is necessary to solve abandonment problems to prevent marriage abandonment. A change of mind can lead to a change in behavior, resulting in a healthier relationship and marriage.

When we meet or date anyone, let's discuss these flu-like symptoms (our responses and fears). What are your secret feelings? Am I good enough? Are you going to love me for who I am? Do you pick the sort of mate you want, or do you accept the invitation because they have sent it to you? Are you entitled to a mistake, or are you guilty?

Finally, do you have a deep reservoir of pain and frustration which you cover with a smile when remaining in an unhealthy relationship? If you answered yes to these questions and had relationship problems or have been abused, that is your reality. And you will learn how to cope with abandonment feelings.

Healing and Eradicating Symptoms

Can I cope in a relationship with abandonment issues? Continuing healing starts with awareness. Everything begins with what you see in yourself, how you view love and marriage, and if you are willing to have more stable relationships and personal emotional wellbeing.

Do you know your triggers? These stimuli can be involuntary at first, but you become very aware of them as you start the process of healing. An event or spoken word is a trigger that sends an emotion of your past that causes you to think and feel those thoughts. Such thoughts and feelings produce a continuum of actions that can be defensive or self-sabotage mechanisms. When you understand these stimuli, you will pause from a clear perspective to analyze your thoughts and emotions. This helps you to respond with a conscious mental filter rather than emotional. It is reality, but we don't always feel our feelings. The more you use this process in your recovery, the more symptoms will be eradicated.

You can now choose joy when you recognize and become receptive to the causes caused by rejection and violence. Now you can make more rational choices in a relationship because the choice is not a need anymore, but a willingness to love and be loved honestly. You decide what you can embrace and what you will deny if you want to be truly loved. You will also benefit from knowing your triggers and how to change your response because you're trying to work by experience, not irrational emotion. I have been in dysfunctional relationships and abusive marriages for many years. I provide details of my feelings and thoughts, and you see them without cuts and honestly. If you are married and decide to have children, then be careful and take this time to understand what you want in a relationship and know that on the other side of recovery, there's joy if you want it.

How to Overcome Fear of Abandonment

It's not fear of giving up; it's how we treat it and undermine our ties. It can conflict with or improve our relationships. Once we can deal with this simple fear, we have access to its healing qualities.

This anxiety is caused by feeling drawn to someone. Most people complain about their loss in a prison of their own making. "I am too weak, too afraid to be in a relationship." We get caught in habits of persistent re-abandoholism or avoid relationships to avoid pain (abandophobism). Some live in a relationship but experience constant confusion and jealousy.

Self-treatment habits are an option. Identify what isn't working:

1. You want so much so fast and have unreasonable aspirations for your partner. You respond over and over, making you and your partner feel less for you and yourself.
2. You're aware that your anxiety pushes your partner away, but you can't find the ability to turn fear away.
3. Try to influence your mate to make it better for you. It raises strain and reduces the quotient of the partnership.
4. Try to hide the emotional cups as rage or covetousness. The vacuum cups specifically target the partner irrespective of how you play them and are heard by the special radar of your partner.
5. Twist yourself up to cover your fear. You lose your credibility in trying to save the relationship.
6. Let your partner feel responsible for you emotionally. It generates the negative situation that you need them more than they need you. This can lead to depression worsening, and a catastrophic loop is created.

7. You loathe when you fear that your partner is causing insecurity.

But don't panic! You can turn it around!

What to do:

1. Avoid beating yourself. It is accidental to fear abandonment. You didn't do it. You didn't sign up for anything. It's not your fault.
2. Consider this fear as part of being a human being. Give yourself unconditional self-love and compassion rather than judging yourself as "weak."
3. Choose to stop putting your fear at the feet of your partner (or anyone else).
4. Instead of asking your partner to "fix," take 100% responsibility when your anxiety erupts.
5. Let us use the fear of abandonment to build emotional self-confidence.
6. Bring your partner for yourself with self-confidence.
7. Be personally interested in the deconstruction of abandonment. The tools can help you handle your own emotional needs in a structured way so that you do not need to rely on your partner.
8. Remember the fact that no one other than you are responsible for making you feel safe. When you look for the answer in your partner, you give away your power.
9. Leap emotional self-assurance but do it on your own. This is not all that we achieve. This is a long, steady, and intermittent path to emotional self-assurance.
10. Only turn if you find yourself looking for reassurance again to your spouse! Get back on the path! Make yourself 100% responsible.
11. Transforming abandonment anxiety into emotional autonomy implies that you embrace your separateness as an individual. It helps you to put a stop to your partner's vulnerability and take responsibility for your emotional needs.

Some Tips for Overcoming Abandonment Issues

Let someone in. Big changes begin with small steps. Teach yourself to trust again-don't worry; this does not have to be serious! Trust in people does not necessarily mean revealing your darkest, deepest secrets; begin by telling friends small things they don't know about your life.

You will improve your connections by sharing knowledge and knowing that people are interested and involved in your life. Over time, you will share more important stuff that you don't find as frightening as you once did. By engaging yourself in sharing, you can think more about people and not always feel so worried.

Confidence is a big step forward in any relationship, from close family members to good friends to the person with whom you are living. If you feel troublesome at first-this is natural; do not judge yourself!

Go at a pace appropriate for you and spend time knowing that you will not be deceived by anyone.

Find an outlet. Seek a comfortable place where you can share your apprehension and anxiety. You do not have to share this with anybody; you can write a diary or set up a blog protected by a password, which helps you to write freely without fear of judgment you feel. Writing down the information also allows us to make things simpler and is a good way to do it all. Journals are a fantastic place to continue if you are still finding it difficult to talk with people about your personal life.

If you feel more comfortable singing or constructing works of art, go for it. You don't have to share that you do it (if you don't want to); just keep it for yourself. Songwriting is a beautiful way to share emotions, and songs from others help us understand how we feel. The concept of being part of a team that has to invest in others can be a good choice too. A sense of community and appreciation can be a nice remembrance of people.

Be responsible for your feelings. Part of working on your mind and all the related stuff (self-confidence, problems of intimacy, and worry) is what you hear. It could be so easy to hide in the safety of denial and not to admit that something feels scary or upsetting, while in the short term, it feels good; it does not help.

CHAPTER 12: HOW DO I REGAIN MY PARTNER

Here, you are going to be working together with your partner to help reconnect. This will help begin to foster that trust and intimacy that may have degraded over time. You must go through this process to ensure that you know not only what you are doing but how you are doing it. It will help you greatly imagine what it is that matters and how you can foster it.

Try Something New for Both of You

The first exercise for you to try is to find something that neither of you has done and work hard to make it happen between both of you. The idea here is that you should both be entirely unfamiliar with what you are about to do. You should both be just as experienced about whatever is happening. It could be that only one of you has any real interest, and that is okay. However, ideally, it would be something that both of you would enjoy doing.

When you find out what you both have never tried together, it is time to make it happen. It is always better if what you are trying is something that will ideally allow for you both to work together-perhaps it is an escape room, which is highly trendy these days and will require teamwork. Maybe you do one of those partner paint activities in which you both paint one half of a scene that is meant to be hung over your bed. No matter what it is that you both decide to do, it should be something that is compelling and brings you both some enjoyment.

After you have tried this new thing together, it is time for you both to talk about it. Talk about how fun it was to experience something together for the first time. Talk about how exciting it was for both of you to get to do something like that and then try to make it happen regularly. You should both try something new often to not only help with your relationship and bonding but also to help with anxiety as well.

Weekly Date Night

Every week, you should have a date night. It does not matter what the date is-but it should be sacred time for just the two of you to spend time together. Perhaps you decide that you are going to have some date nights at home, and this is fine, too. You do not have to break the bank to have this special time reserved. It could be just as special to cook a nice, special meal, share some wine, and watch a new movie together as it is to go out to a fancy restaurant.

What matters here, however, is the prioritization of the relationship. Make sure that you are actively putting your relationship first as much as you can to ensure that you are properly taking care of it. It is up to the two of you to maintain your relationship, and this is one of the best ways to bring that intimacy and connection back if you have lost touch with it.

Spend Time Together Every Day

Make every single day that passes a point to stop and spend some time together. It could be that you stop and eat dinner together every night. It could be that you spend some time chatting with your partner in bed without any distractions. It could be that you spend ten minutes each morning cuddling in bed before you get up to face the day, or you spend that time together at night.

There are all sorts of ways to spend time with your partner, even if you are on the go or if you cannot be with each other physically. On the go, you could hold hands in the car as one of you drives, or you could spend time talking, face to face, on a video call if you live too far apart to spend time together regularly. Spend that time together and enjoy that quiet moment together.

Trust Falls

This one may seem kind of doubtful to you-no one likes the idea of falling. However, trust falls are legitimately good for your relationship. Your partner should be the first person that you go to when you need something. When you need help, they should be the one that pops into mind. They should be that support for you that you know that you need to ensure that you can get that help that is required, and the best way to ensure that you have that is through the use of exercises like this.

The trust fall is meant to be something that will work to establish that trust. Essentially, what you are going to do is stop, lean back, and then allow for the fall to happen. The other person should be right behind your back and ready to catch you when you start to fall. This is essential to ensuring that support for each other. When you do this, and when you blindly fall backward, trusting your partner, you will begin to build that trust up. And, if you somehow manage to fall together, you can laugh and make a joke about it and move on.

Gratitude List

One last exercise for you to consider is the gratitude list. We all have things in our lives that we are grateful for. We may be grateful that we have food in the fridge or power or a roof over our heads. However, how often do you stop and think about everything that you are grateful for about your partner? What is it that happens when you stop to think about what your partner does for you or how your partner can help you? Stop and consider this for a few moments, and then write it all down into a list that you can share with him or her.

The idea here is that you will be able to tell the other person exactly what you appreciate about them. They will do the same for you, and this means that you will be able to recognize the truth of the matter. You will be able to get those feelings into words in front of you, and your partner will be able to see them written out for him or her as well, and vice versa.

When you can see that your partner truly does appreciate you and respect you, you can start to feel much better and much more confident in the relationship. You will be able to process how you can interact with them-you will see the fact that your relationship is not one-sided when you realize that there were things that your partner also appreciated about you. This helps build confidence as well-you and your partner will both likely feel much better when you realize how much you mean to each other!

CHAPTER 13: LEARN HOW TO MANAGE EMOTIONS

To truly master your emotions, you will need to go a lot further than just engaging in sporadic emotional management practices anytime emotion is triggered within you. You will need to be willing to intentionally work with your emotions every day so that you can acknowledge, process, and release your emotions on a day-to-day basis. In doing so, you are allowing yourself to release your emotional reserves to not hold onto them longer than necessary. You also allow yourself to create space for yourself to learn from your emotions and discover new ways to deal with them more healthily and productively.

As you will discover over time, your emotions are something that you will continually learn from every single day. The process of learning how to navigate emotions healthily and productively lasts a lifetime, largely because every time an emotion is triggered, it will be under different circumstances. The more emotion is triggered, especially under different circumstances, the more you become aware of how those emotions feel for you and how you can navigate those emotions more effectively.

There are many ways that you can create a daily emotional management ritual for yourself, with no one answer being right or wrong. The key to finding a ritual that works best for you is to identify what your life tends to look like from an emotional point of view and to create a ritual that works best for you. An ideal ritual should address how you feel and help you learn from and release those emotions all at once. If you are dealing with a particularly troubling emotion, your daily ritual should include some form of activity intended to help you process that emotion, too. This way, you are always working within your needs and supporting your overall and day-to-day emotional wellbeing.

Stay Committed to Your Daily Mindfulness Ritual

The first thing you can do for yourself, from an emotional capacity, is staying committed to your daily mindfulness ritual. Mindfulness is going to help you in countless ways, including processing and releasing emotions. A great way to incorporate mindfulness specifically into your daily emotional management ritual is to use mindfulness to help you recognize what emotions you are experiencing and to navigate them in an intentional capacity. The more mindful you are, the more you will find meaningful ways to address your emotions during your emotional release.

One great way to incorporate mindfulness into your emotional management routine is to take the time to investigate any emotions you have experienced throughout your day mindfully. You can start by noticing one to three emotions you may have experienced that day that was particularly strong for you. Do not work through any more than three at a time, though, as you do not want to overwhelm yourself and make it more challenging for you to address your emotions.

Once you have noticed these emotions, give yourself time to analyze why they occurred, what happened once they did, and how the aftermath of those emotions was experienced. If you can identify the trigger of the emotions, understand your thoughts and feelings in response to those emotions, and recognize how they lead to your behavior. This will give you a greater understanding of how those emotions affected you. Likewise, if you can acknowledge your "emotions" consequences, you can create the opportunity for you to understand how your emotional responses affected you in the long run. Be sure to do this for both negative and positive emotions, as this will give you a chance to identify opportunities for growth while also giving you a chance to celebrate yourself for the growth you have already implemented.

Take Up Journaling

Journaling is a wonderful practice for many different reasons. Aside from helping you keep a little log of your life, journaling allows you to express your true thoughts and emotions outside of yourself, where you otherwise may not have been able to. Many people talk about what they truly think and feel seems impossible, even if they are talking to someone such as a therapist where it seems like you "should" be able to speak honestly about what you are thinking or feeling. Having a private journal that you keep to yourself can be a great way for you to openly admit to how you were truly feeling, what you were truly thinking, and anything else that you may have hidden during your day. You can also honestly reflect on what you think and feel after the fact.

Releasing your thoughts from your mind and physically getting them out onto paper may not be quite the same as talking to someone about your emotions, but it will provide you with a great opportunity to get a sense of release. In many cases, the sooner you can release your feelings by admitting them, and the more honestly you can do so, the easier it will be for you to let go and move on in the long run. However, if you get into the habit of acknowledging your emotions and then repressing them, it will become more challenging for you to release how you feel about that particular situation. Hence, the pent-up experience begins.

If you are not someone who typically journals, rest assured that there does not need to be a right way or a wrong way for you to engage in journaling. You do not have to be thoughtful, emotional, curious, or well-articulated to keep a journal. You also do not need to worry about spelling, grammar, punctuation, or other writing errors. You don't even need to worry about writing full-form sentences, sharing things in story form, or otherwise being exhaustive in what you are thinking and feeling. Even just keeping bullet-point-styled notes about what you were thinking and feeling and how that impacted you can be plenty to help you sort through what is going on in your brain. Use your journal in a way that works for you, and trust that this will be plenty to help you fully accept, learn from, and release any emotions you have experienced on a day-to-day basis.

Give Yourself Frequent Stress Breaks

I firmly believe that stress breaks should be a mandatory part of everyone's daily activities. Day to day life can be stressful, even if you are doing the same thing every day. The demands of work-life, family life and other parts of life can all be overwhelming, even on the best of days. Giving yourself stress breaks means that you are willing to acknowledge your emotional state and make choices that will nurture your wellbeing. When it comes to emotional management, there is no one-size-fits-all. Spending just one session working on your emotions each day will not result in you having effortless or healthy emotional expressions for the rest of the day. It will improve your chances. However, you still need to make choices that will keep you in a healthy state of expression during the day. You can improve your expressions on a day-to-day basis by being willing to give yourself stress breaks so that you can decompress.

A stress break could be an intentionally scheduled break where you get to do something different from your normal activities. However, a stress break can also be accomplished by giving yourself 5-10 minutes to decompress anytime you find yourself feeling particularly stressed or emotionally charged during the day. You can also give yourself 5-10 minutes to decompress if you find yourself feeling drained or overdrawn from your day. During those 5-10 minutes, allow yourself time to simply breathe, be mindful, and engage in a relaxing routine that will allow you to feel more at peace after your day. Through this, you will find yourself flowing much more peacefully and harmoniously throughout your day.

Work in Harmony with Your Nature

Whenever you try to do something, it is always best to work with your nature rather than against it. In particular, with emotions, working with your nature means rather than denying your emotions or trying to force them to change, you learn to incorporate them into your daily experience. Incorporating your emotions into your daily routines could include fitting certain parts of your routines into certain parts of your day and scheduling your days based on how your feelings behave.

When it comes to scheduling with your energy, consider how you tend to have energy during the day and schedule your activities based on that. This way, you are not trying to force yourself to engage in things when you do not have adequate energy for them. Therefore, you have no reason to feel pressured or stressed in those activities. For example, if you know that you tend to have more energy in the morning and less in the evening, you could exercise in the morning and do your mindfulness routine in the evening. If, however, you are the opposite and you tend to have less energy in the morning and more in the evening, you might benefit from doing your mindfulness practice in the morning and exercising in the evening. This way, you are working with your nature to create harmony and flow throughout your day, and you are not amplifying your stress for any reason.

You can also schedule your days based on how you anticipate you will feel. For example, let's say you are trying to schedule your week out, and you know that you have a stressful project to complete on Tuesday. Based on this knowledge, you might make Monday and Tuesday relatively relaxing days and save other things, such as cleaning the house or engaging in other demanding activities later, once the project has already been finished. This way, rather than forcing yourself to get anything done when you already know that you won't have the energy, you work with your nature instead.

As far as emotional fulfillment efforts go, focus on learning tools that allow you to release emotions in a way that can easily be executed on a day-to-day basis. Exercise, art, listening to music, relaxing, talking to a loved one, and other similar measures can all be used to release your emotions in a healthy, productive manner. Suppose you tend to experience many rapid emotions during the day. In that case, you might even consider carrying a journal with you and quickly jotting things down anytime you come across a large feeling. This way, you can quickly release that feeling at the moment, and you can reasonably circle back to it later on in the day. This would be far healthier than, say, stuffing it down and allowing it to ruin the rest of your day.

CHAPTER 14: DEVELOP CONFIDENCE AND SELF-ESTEEM TO OVERCOME INSECURITIES

There are several strategies that you can implement to enhance your self-confidence and boost your self-esteem. Here are some of them.

- **Re-affirm your positive traits:** Just as we often think negative things about ourselves, we must learn to affirm positive traits as well. For example, maybe you're constantly telling yourself, "You're a lazy person." You've been telling yourself that for so long that you believe it, and you've internalized that voice. To see yourself positively and improve your self-esteem, try telling yourself the opposite.
- **Avoid comparisons:** One of the toughest parts of developing your self-esteem is realizing that you cannot compare yourself to others. Too often, we compare ourselves with people around us like family, co-workers, friends, or people we don't even know, thanks to the exposure to social media. Whether it's about looks, money, personal possessions, or whatever it may be, the trap of comparing is that you never feel good enough.
- **Identify your unique gifts:** Everyone has something that they excel at. We all have our strengths and our weaknesses. Instead of focusing on your weaknesses, focus on what your strengths are and what skills you possess that make you feel confident. Whether it's your skills at work, your creative outlets, your skill on the guitar, or how well you cook, it's important that you are not ashamed of what you do well and channel that energy so you feel confident about yourself. Don't focus on your failures-focus on your successes! Be proud of your accomplishments.
- **Focus on self-care:** Whether you are exercising, treating yourself to a spa day, or getting a good night's sleep, you must take care of yourself physically to take care of your mental health. Exercise is proven to release serotonin, a neurotransmitter of the brain that creates feelings of happiness and contentment. Whether it's an hour at the gym or just going for an evening walk before dinner, take some time to exercise, so you are physically taking care of

yourself. Do something relaxing for yourself after a long week. Treat yourself to a cheat day if you've been sticking to your diet regularly. Whatever it is, you should focus on yourself and making your emotional and mental health a priority.

- **Help others:** Studies show that helping someone else or volunteering can help you feel better about yourself. It takes you out of your mindset and urges you to think about someone else. The best way to increase your feelings of self-worth is volunteering face-to-face, such as at a homeless shelter or a soup kitchen. But if you can also donate money or provide services online, then you can also increase your self-worth. You can feel like you are part of a cause and that you are helping people. You have a purpose. This gives value to you and your time, and you feel part of a greater community. This increases your self-worth and self-esteem and how you feel about yourself.
- **Remind yourself that you are not your circumstances:** Tell yourself over and over that even if you are going through a tough time right now, you may not be soon. Circumstances occur in our life that is sometimes out of our control. As the saying goes, "this, too, shall pass." With hard work, compassion, and patience, whatever tough time you are going through will soon ease itself. Your problems will be solved, and you will feel stronger for having gone through them. This is important to recognize your self-esteem and not let the circumstances around you beat you down.

CHAPTER 15: TIPS FOR A LONG AND HAPPY RELATIONSHIP

The following tips will help keep your relationship healthy for a long time.

Avoid Nagging

Any kind of criticism of your partner's idiosyncrasies either leads to quarrels or makes you feel annoyed. Psychologists think that criticizing your partner in many cases is a projection of your shortcomings.

Rather than frustrating your partner with complaints, you might think about what makes you uncomfortable about their traits and work on reframing your viewpoint.

Understand That Your Partner Is Their Personality

You must accept the fact that your partner is an individual with a unique personality. Nevertheless, we subconsciously and sometimes consciously treat our partners as if they are an extension of ourselves. Accept that your partner is a being with a character of their own, with appropriate feelings and perceptions, opinions, and experiences.

Accept Your Partner's Mistakes

To err is human. Your partner is not an angel, so they are bound to make mistakes. When that happens, learn to forgive and do not capitalize on the mistakes of your partner.

Above all, there are lots of things we cannot change about our partner, so rather than grumbling or nagging, why not learn to live with them? Small mistakes are not a matter of life and death. If you find it difficult to cope with your partner's idiosyncrasies, call their attention to it, and politely explain yourself. Don't blame or accuse; simply discuss.

Be Honest

Honesty is the best policy. Not only is this concept over two centuries old, but it exactly hits the point where relationships can fail.

Half-truths and lies cannot be kept secret for long if you aim to live peacefully together with your partner. Also, do not hide any material facts that could have a direct impact on the growing relationship. For example, if you have children from a previous relationship, that's something that will have to come out eventually.

Be Faithful and Sincere

Unless you have made other arrangements, share a duvet exclusively with your romantic partner and no one else. To be deceived and cheated on by a close person is one of the cruelest experiences that can happen to anyone.

If you love your partner, you will spare them that experience. Ultimately, faithfulness builds such deep trust that you can't replace or fix it once broken.

Address Problems

No partnership is in complete harmony. You are two different personalities with thoughts and feelings. A relationship, no matter how much love and dedication you feel for each other, is always the result of many compromises.

Instead of holding long-standing resentments, you should discuss issues openly with your partner and work together to find a solution without immediately interpreting them as signs of a nonfunctional relationship. Precisely because you can talk about difficult points, you have a strong partnership.

Appreciate What You See in Your Partner

The first infatuation does not disappear forever. Most of the time, it gives way only to another feeling, that too, of deep attachment and love.

You have found that you can rely on your partner and that they think of you, and in so many ways suit you perfectly, and that you as a couple harmonize and like to be with one another.

Romantic Excursions

Enjoy your closeness and take out time for romantic excursions from everyday life. Take a nice walk in the fall or have a special dinner together in the evening. Everyday life can dull the magic that is created while being with another person. Get away from the routine to rediscover your partner. For a relationship to work, you have to do a lot for it.

CHAPTER 16: TECHNIQUES TO MAINTAIN INTIMACY

When relationships start to go south, the first thing to go in the relationship is intimacy. Intimacy encompasses a range of connections in your relationship. It references your emotional connection, your sex life, and the level of closeness between you and your partner. Intimacy fosters closeness and enables a couple to be comfortable enough with each other to open up about their innermost desires and emotions.

Sex is much more than just a physical act. It requires two people to be willing to open up to each other and be vulnerable. Have you noticed that when you are mad at your partner, you have trouble getting intimate with them? Contrary to popular belief, it is not that easy to separate your physical relationship from your emotional one.

The more loved and appreciated you feel, the more open you are to intimacy. This just means that when a relationship is going well, you probably have a healthy emotional connection and a healthy sex life. Both parties feel that their emotional and physical needs are being met. One of the biggest mistakes you can make in a relationship is to use intimacy as a weapon.

Some people resort to withdrawing affection as a way of punishing or manipulating their partner. When you use such tactics, you are undermining the value of intimacy in your relationship. It becomes less about connecting with your partner intimately and more about controlling the other person.

Maintaining intimacy and keeping the passion alive is one of how you can strengthen your relationship. When you neglect this aspect of your relationship, you start to lose some of the closeness that keeps couples bonded to each other. Intimacy communicates your affection to the other person. It makes your partner feel valued when you show them that you are still interested in them.

One of the main issues that may affect intimacy in your relationship is the inability to communicate your needs and desires to your partner. Most people are afraid to discuss any issues that they feel are too intimate such as sex. For some, it could be due to the fear of getting hurt, while others are simply not comfortable with the vulnerability that comes with opening up their innermost feelings. When this happens, one or both partners can become dissatisfied with the relationship.

Open communication means that you are free to express your needs and open up to your partner. It also means that you are also ready to hear your partner out on their needs without judgment and with an open mind. Do not be afraid to spice things up in the bedroom. Finding new ways to satisfy each other is one of the most romantic things you can do for your relationship.

Let your partner know how they make you feel and encourage them to express how they feel as well. The more you know about what pleases your partner, the better you get at meeting their needs. Avoid getting into a rut by exploring new things and getting in touch with your adventurous side.

Let your partner know that you are thinking about them throughout the day. Intimacy is not just about sex; enjoy being close and cuddling as a way of bonding. Even when you are not in the mood, you can still show your partner affection by kissing or holding them close as you sleep.

Nobody likes to feel rejected. Even when you are not willing to get intimate, be kind to your partner, and explain your feelings to them. If your partner starts to feel rejected, they will shy away from initiating intimacy because they do not want to be turned down. Knowing how to communicate with the other person without hurting their feelings will help you keep your intimate relationship healthy.

Tips for Maintaining Intimacy in Your Relationship

1. Spend time together. The closer you feel to your partner, the better the emotional and physical connection that you will have with them. Make time to have deep conversations and talk to each other.
2. Break the routine. Surprise your partner with a weekend gate away, sign up for a class together or take up a new hobby together. It doesn't matter what the activity is; just make some effort to break away from your normal routine and do something new together. This is a great way to reconnect and find out new things about each other

3. Avoid being judgmental or critical. Your partner should feel safe opening up to you with their innermost feelings and desires. This will help you to become closer and feel free to open up with each other without the fear of being hurt or judged.
4. Be affectionate with your partner. Holding hands, kissing, and other displays of affection all help to foster intimacy and the sense of closeness it brings. When you show affection, it communicates your feelings and expresses your interest in the other person.
5. Reminisce and share memories of things that made you happy or experiences that have made you come closer. Just talking about happy memories has an instant effect on how close you feel to each other. Pull out the old photo albums, watch your wedding videos, or just have a laugh about some adventure in your past. It will help you reconnect and foster intimacy in your relationship.
6. Create a wind-down routine for the two of you at the end of each day. It can be going to bed at the same time so that you can catch up on each other's day or having some quiet time just the two of you after dinner.

CHAPTER 17: DEALING WITH A NARCISSISTIC PARTNER

Life with a Narcissistic Partner or Spouse

Nobody's family can be perfect. There are always differences, and working things out is par for the course. But when your partner or spouse experiences NPD, it can appear to be nearly difficult to work things out. As a partner or spouse, individuals with NPD regularly show the following sorts of behaviors:

- Demand to be the main important individual, commanding constant regard and admiration, in any event, demanding to be picked above the children who may be viewed as contenders for your attention
- Seem to have next to zero regards for your boundaries, feelings, or needs and doesn't appreciate your separateness in the relationship
- Experts in temptation and manipulation in requests to get a partner to do what they wish; narcissists may utilize sex as a substitute for intimacy or love. If you presume that you are living with a narcissist, watch all the intimate minutes you share and notice which-if any-are not sexual. If they are almost all sexual, your narcissist may be using the act to avoid real intimacy.

Individuals with NPD may or may not know exactly how their dis-request is affecting their behaviors, although they may have an idea that something isn't right. They may realize that they like to be regarded, adored, and admired. But except if they have a background themselves in psychology or have had some therapy, they may not so much understand their feelings or behaviors. They don't accept analysis in any kind of reasonable way. Pointing out bad habits or behaviors is a "no-no" with narcissists, although this would be an important part of working out most other intimate relationships. Statements that don't affirm their perfection are perceived as an attack, and they may lash out brutally. Regardless of whether in the beginning, they got things done to intrigue you when they begin to feel they are not getting the stock they need, their behaviors will change because of their frustrations and may include raging, abandoning, sulking, quiet treatment, risky behaviors, humiliating, belittling, conceivably becoming abusive, and in any case devaluing you. If their abilities in their jobs, diversions, or activities don't fulfill their guidelines-for example, losing at sports, receiving analysis at work, or not getting advancement-their frustration is regularly transferred to you, their nearest relationship. Or on the other hand, frustrations can be transferred into harmful activities, including drugs, drinking, gambling, and wild spending. A narcissist that was passed over for advancement or struck out at a baseball game may return home and berate you for reasons unknown or go out drinking-anything to get back that sense of control.

Sometimes narcissists can do the inverse; they return home and lament that they're nothing more than trouble, they behave badly, and so on. They are looking for you to protect them and reveal to them how superb they are. And if you are mutually dependent or enamored with your narcissist, you probably will fill their narcissistic stock.

What You May Be Feeling and Finding

- You may feel you have to take the necessary steps to balance your relationship with your partner or spouse.
- You may find yourself questioning what you fouled up to cause a change in the individual and attempt all ways to fix the situation.
- There may be a snapshot of believing that behaviors have gone back to the way they were at the beginning of the relationship, renewing your expectations and canceling out the realities of unhealthy, inefficient situations that have continued for quite a while.
- You may feel lost and confounded, not knowing what is the real truth or not.
- You may find that the narcissist has left you and discovered someone else, usually not feeling they have done anything incorrectly or caring to dwell on anything negative.

Dealing with a Narcissistic Partner or Spouse

Here are some pointers to consider for yourself, regardless of whether you choose to stay in a relationship with a narcissist and for how long:

- Because he probably has difficulty expressing necessities and feelings to you, it tends to be useful for you to demonstrate the communication skills of identifying feelings by starting your statements with "I believe," "I felt when you," "I'd like you to do"

- You may wish to attempt what's called active listening. After he says something, repeat what he said with "Did I hear you right? You want me to do XYZ?" This doesn't mean you agree with what he said; you are simply validating him and showing that you are listening to him.

One method that can better interact is to take your own space or timeouts when you need them. Rather if you sense the beginning of contention, just say, "It doesn't seem as though we can talk about this at present, so I'm going to take a brief break and continue later." Then go to another room, take a walk-take charge of your situation.

- You may attempt to detach from feeling answerable for what the narcissist is saying or doing or not doing. Regardless of whether you gave him each and everything he wanted from you, he would probably still not be satisfied and content.
- You may attempt to learn to accept and release it and not feel that you must experience the high points and low points with him.
- You may attempt to avoid paying attention to his twisted perspective on you, for example, "It's your fault, you're selfish, you don't understand, you try not to adore me."

CHAPTER 18: HOW TO TREAT THE EMOTIONAL WOUNDS OF A COUPLE'S BREAKUP

One of the hardest things anyone will ever have to do is to end a relationship. Whether it is a family relationship, a marriage, or even just a friendship, every relationship is sacred as it fills a special place in a person's heart. This is why codependent relationships are so devastating. They tear away at a person's heart day by day until there is nothing left but pain and misery. Unfortunately, to escape that pain and misery, a person may have to end a relationship, no matter how intimate or long-lived it may be. Although the decision to end a relationship can be painful, the act itself doesn't have to be overly devastating.

Recognize the Decision Is Yours

When it comes to ending a relationship, perhaps the most important thing to remember is that the decision is yours. You alone have chosen to remain in the relationship, and you alone are now deciding to bring it to an end. While this may seem to add a significant burden of guilt on your shoulders, especially in the case where the other person appears devastated from the decision, it also adds an element of control that is critically important. More often than not, the other person in the relationship will fight to maintain the union, thereby maintaining control over you. However, by recognizing that the decision to leave is yours, you can prevent them from taking the decision away from you.

Needless to say, such an act should never be taken lightly; therefore, it is important to take the time to weigh all factors involved when reaching this final choice carefully. However, once you have made up your mind to end a relationship, the important thing is to trust the decision you are making. If you allow yourself to second guess things, especially in light of any arguments that the other person might have or of any sympathy you might feel toward them, your resolve will begin to waiver, creating doubt, confusion, and even guilt in your heart and mind. These are the tools that a codependent person will use to gain control over another person; therefore, you need to protect yourself from them at all costs. Subsequently, once you decide to end a relationship, you need to trust that you are making the right choice, and you need to see the process through to the end, only then you can regain the control over your life that is necessary for building the healthy and happy life you both desire and deserve.

Have the Conversation

For one thing, it suggests that the other person doesn't deserve a face-to-face conversation in which they can speak their piece. After all, a letter is essentially a one-sided conversation; thus, it forces one person's opinion on the other. Therefore, to be fair, it is best to have a conversation where both sides can have their say.

Choosing the right location for such a conversation is critical, as this detail alone can significantly affect the nature of the conversation itself. If you have it in a place where the other person feels in control, they will try to take over the conversation, thereby changing the course of events in their favor. Alternatively, if you place them in a strange environment where they feel out of control, it can cause them to become overly defensive, closing off to you in every way. While this may not be the worst thing, especially in the case of ending a relationship, it can still add pain and suffering that can be avoided. The best option is to choose a place that is familiar to both parties, but that doesn't give an advantage to either. A place that is both public yet somewhat private, such as a quiet corner in a park or on a beach, can be a perfect choice; here, you can have a private conversation without feeling intimidated, trapped, or on display.

This is important since the emotional nature of the event will be so strong that it can easily scramble anyone's mind. The last thing you want to do is stumble over the points you want to make, or even worse, forget many of them altogether. Therefore, you must write down those points so that you can refer to them if your mind begins to cloud over. That said, you don't have to write a speech as such, reading word for word as if you were holding a press conference. Instead, list the topics you want to cover as though you were writing a grocery list. You can even check off each item as you cover it to keep track of the progress of the conversation in addition to ensuring you stay on point with the things you want to discuss; having this list will also eliminate the stress of trying to remember everything can cause. Now, instead of having to memorize your lines for a performance, you can have a flexible conversation, one that allows for heartfelt discussion from all sides and that still ensures you get your points across.

Avoid Placing Blame or Guilt

No one ever ends a relationship for good reasons. You wouldn't end a marriage because you were having too much fun, or you felt too loved. Nor would you end a friendship because your friend was too nice to you. Instead, you choose to end relationships with people who bring pain, suffering, and misery into your life. As a result, it can be all too tempting to fill the relationship ending a conversation with accusations, blame, and guilt, thereby attacking the other person as though they are on trial. At the same time, this may seem like a good way to bring closure by releasing all of your anger and frustration; it can backfire, causing you to feel guilty long after the relationship is ended. Therefore, to avoid causing more pain than necessary, both for yourself as well as the other person, you must avoid placing blame or guilt on the other person in the course of your conversation with them.

A good way to achieve this goal is to avoid focusing on the past. While it may seem logical to focus on the reasons for ending a relationship, such as the actions and behaviors of the other person that caused you pain and suffering, this will only come across as accusatory in the end. A better approach is to focus on the future. After all, you aren't ending the relationship just to get away from the codependent behaviors that are causing you harm; you are ending the relationship to a fresh start, healthy, and happy life for yourself. Thus, rather than focusing on the dark past that you are breaking free from, you should focus on your future hopes and dreams, those things you are moving toward. This will put a positive spin on the conversation, avoiding the negative aspects of anger, blame, and guilt.

You can treat it like you would if you were putting in your notice at work. Anytime you quit a job, it's because you are usually unhappy with the job you have. When you put in your notice, you can rant and rave about how badly you have been treated, or you can choose to tell your boss that you are ready for new challenges or that a job you have always wanted has become available. In the end, it is always best to live and let live. Once you end the relationship, you will be free from the codependent behaviors and influences that caused you pain, and that is all that counts. Therefore, focus on the positive future rather than the negative past. While the process of ending a relationship will be painful, it doesn't have to be traumatic. By staying as positive as possible, you will ensure that the pain and suffering experienced by everyone involved remain as minimal as possible.

Remain Calm and Compassionate

Again, this may not be an easy thing to do, especially if the other person reacts in a highly emotional way. And since they are codependent, this is probably a very safe bet. Fortunately, there are a couple of tricks that can help you to keep calm, even in the worst-case scenario. One is to treat the conversation as a done deal. In other words, this isn't a negotiation in which one side or the other will come out the winner. This is a decision that you have already made; therefore, you have already won. The outcome is already decided. The future is already written. Therefore, you don't have anything to worry about. You don't have to get drawn into an argument as there is nothing to prove or gain as a result. Instead, you just have to deliver the message that you are moving on with your life.

Another trick to help you remain calm and compassionate is to recognize that aggressive behavior is usually a sign of pain. Therefore, if the other person flies off on a tangent, ranting and raving about all of the things you have done or how bad you are as a person, rather than arguing back, simply recognize that they are crying out in pain. If you react in an emotionally charged way, you will only increase that pain and suffering, making you a monster in the process. You aren't a monster, which is why you want to end your codependent relationships. Therefore, act like the decent, loving person you are and be ever-compassionate no matter what. See this act of love and compassion as the first step toward your newfound happy and healthy life.

Be Firm

Finally, when it comes to ending a relationship, you must be firm. Stand by your decision, no matter how much the other person argues, begs, or even threatens. You have decided to move on with your life, and nothing should undermine your conviction to do so. Therefore, be strong, be confident, and most importantly, be firm in your decision to end the relationship.

Being firm doesn't mean that you have to be mean or aggressive; it simply means that you have made up your mind and you need to stick to the choice that you have made. If you allow yourself to be dissuaded from your decision, you can find yourself sliding down the slippery slope that leads back to codependency. Therefore, staying firm isn't about being stubborn or even right; rather, it's about doing the right thing for yourself. That process starts with removing yourself from toxic environments, such as codependent relationships, and putting yourself in more positive environments instead, ones that promote healthy, happy relationships as well as a healthy and happy sense of self-worth.

CHAPTER 19: GETTING OVER RELATIONSHIP INSECURITY AND OBSTACLES IN YOUR RELATIONSHIP

There are moments when the relationship feels uncomfortable. You may feel frustrated. You not only have to control your partnership; you do have to handle external stressors as well. Both associations surpass peaks and lows. What is essential in your relationship is that you can take the lows. You have to know that relationships go through stages. When you get past one hump, there's bound to be a chance you're going to run up against another. You should fix issues in the partnership without breaking up.

Passion requires effort is a pretty general belief. Yet 80 percent of Americans under 30 believe in a soulmate, only waiting to be discovered, thinking that there is a better human out there. Just the word "fallen in love" makes us feel like life is out of our hands-that it only happens to us. It typically isn't easy to find long-lasting love, except though we encounter the right guy. It's also not an excessively laborious job, though, but it sucks up more complicated than it gives of enjoyment. And how do we decide when to give up on friendship, and how do we choose when to struggle for the partnership?

We will then perceive that associations are always delivered complex, even though they can be generally exquisite and agreeable all by themselves. For any two individuals with two different heads, two separate fields, and two different gear sets meet up. What's to come isn't probably going to be only one smooth sail into the dusk. The most pleasant inclination in an individual's life can be becoming hopelessly enamored, yet we keep ignoring the measure of fear, uneasiness, distress, and even fury it can raise.

Through a perverse twist, the closest we come to someone else, those worries continue to grow ever higher. We still have defenses in us without realizing it, centered on hurtful past encounters that even work to drive the love out.

And when it comes to knowing whether to terminate a once cherished relationship, the first question that we have to ask ourselves is how well my defenses are at work? What am I taking closeness to the table that might be sabotaging?

It is necessary to follow the mentality that the only one you will influence is yourself while considering the steps you will take when you agree to split up. You control 100 percent of the dynamics on your part. Despite your friendship, you are not a victim; you will both opt to pass on in the end. Playing the role of guilt will leave you feeling helpless and walking around in circles. And if you finally agree that it is not worth maintaining the friendship as long as you're in it, you can practice being the best individual you can be. You will build your capacity to love, be transparent, and be vulnerable-skills that can profoundly help you in life and relationships to come. To help you heal your friendship, you have to acquire and exercise specific skills in order. Before we say goodbye to the company, here are five items to do with that in mind. The positive thing is being able to benefit from the errors. This is what they term lectures. Now let's think about the techniques and suggestions that will help you overcome partnership problems.

Talk It Out

If you start having issues, it's convenient not to think about them. I should have one partner as a speaker when I see a couple and one as a listener. It is essential that you not only speak about your issues but that you listen. This ensures you have no interruptions and you have no mobile phone. It is how you feel that your partner is attentive. These let us realize that you worry about your partner and that you've got your partner back. Begin the talk about what's happening in the partnership now. Instead, tell your partner what your partner appreciates. That has to be real. This is the position where the smallest stuff creates a huge difference. Being truthful, too, is relevant. That does not mean that you've had to damage the emotions of your partner. Nevertheless, having your partner know how you feel and what you need in the partnership is vital.

Let Go of Your Expectations

You may hope to see stuff moving in some direction. When it's the case, it will push you off. Note, even because the relationship has improved, so everything has it? If you aspire, so anticipate things to shift.

That needn't be evil. Let go of exactly what's right. There's no best direction the mate should be, or the partnership should be. That implies letting go of the "should" block. When people dictate to you how your collaboration will function in your life, it might be time to let go of them. It works for one partnership; for another, it cannot fit.

Stop the Comparison Game

It may sound as if everyone else has a better relationship right now. Yet maybe this is not the case. Most citizens are not concerned about their issues with the partnerships. That indicates you are unable to assess a journal by its cover. When you look at social networking, this occurs. Most people show the best side of their relationship and respect their life, which results in your relationship feelings of loneliness. Note, there is the stuff that you would like in a partnership. Other people don't. So, that's good. It's your partnership, which is significant. Let go of what other people say. That just makes things worse.

Make Sure You Both Compromise

A balance in the partnership is something you still feel comfortable about. I gain we fail / we lose the situation because you disagree, then you build the problem. This would produce a wedge in the connection as time goes by. This is also defined as the start to end. It is where you will, indeed, attempt. When you're not coming to a consensus right away, that's perfect. You should still decide to start up the topic after the date. Be alert not to let that run over the emotions. Be sure you have enough time until you continue to work for a solution. That's not as horrible as it does seem. When you think about your partner, in the end, all of you will feel fine.

Make Sure You Both Feel Safe

It is vital that both of you feel safe emotionally. When you can't communicate your emotions, otherwise, the relationship isn't safe. It's essential to learn your partner appreciates your feelings. For specific individuals, this may be extremely challenging. You could not have grown up in a home where voicing your feelings was free. Or maybe everybody only held their feelings inside. That will leave you feeling trapped when you do this. This can also build a safety net for the partnership as all parties can healthily communicate their emotions.

There is still pair counseling when everything fails. Even if you believe these suggestions support you, you may want to see a pair of therapists. Getting a third party facilitates things. This is someone who can listen and help lead you through this phase without taking sides. Couple counseling can further enhance connectivity, which can help with the relationship's friendship and intimacy. Often, couple counseling is a position where you can tell, "I don't know what to do." Make sure you choose a couple of therapists with whom you will be comfortable and that you can interact.

Reflect on What Drew You Together

We don't necessarily pick partners for the right reasons. We choose people often who question us, who drive us to develop and broaden our universes. On most occasions, we pick individuals whose protections and derogatory attributes match with ours. E.g., if we prefer to be passive or indecisive, we may select someone pushy and assertive. Such characteristics that pull us in the first time can become why we end up dropping out. Sadly, the sparkly attraction we sense is not always a positive indication at the outset.

This could draw on our history-a divisive pattern from our experience that we are subconsciously seeking to reinforce. E.g., suppose we were invisible in our homes. In that case, we could be waiting for a common situation with a spouse who is not displaying any initial concern, who doesn't consider us a priority or express their affections. When we have a parent that wished to "improve us," we may have partners to "support us," but we then come after to hate them for treating us still as the issue that needs to be solved or mastered.

Although our partner's range will often be wrong, it is not necessarily to blame for a partnership's demise. If the appeal and anticipation we feel initially start to disappear, it doesn't automatically imply we have selected the wrong person. This is why awareness of our early feelings in the partnership is so critical. When, at one point, we were genuinely in love with somebody, we will recover those feelings. We should consider what attracted us to our companion and the years of mutual experience in which we experienced interaction, love, and intimacy. Instead, we will search at the real causes of why things have taken a turn for the worse and create a transition that can lead us closer to those original emotions and have a positive effect.

Try Breaking Your Routine

One of the key reasons a partnership falls is that the pair have formed a "Fantasy Bond." A Fantasy Bond is a word used at some stage in their collaboration to explain an impression of attachment that couples experience. A Fantasy Relationship varies from true love. Heartfelt gestures of compassion are substituted by ritual, and type in comparison is preferred over the material. Couples join this situation without really knowing it as a way of experiencing a false sense of comfort, an impression of fusion or "oneness." A Fantasy Bond has a "deadening" impact on a partnership.

Two spouses tend to dominate one another and restrict one another's perceptions. They are a "we," although they lack a sense of each of their origins as two different individuals. Apparent interaction is reduced; only intimate interactions give and take. Partners take each other for granted and lack each other's passion. We stop supporting the specific interests and traits of personality that illuminate the other individual and make them who they are. In effect, that generates a staled partnership atmosphere in which all sides experience frustration and loss of interest in each other.

Several aspects of a Fantasy Bond are worth investigating but note that this relationship is not a black or white state. There remains a Fantasy Relationship within a line. Many people, having formed an association of different degrees, consider themselves somewhere in the continuum. We will start breaking free of imagination by adjusting the way we connect in our partnership. You will follow this approach by deciding to take more responsibility in your collaboration, rather than passively, with whatever your spouse wants. You should do this on your own, without your partner doing it.

CHAPTER 20: HABITS OF A SUCCESSFUL COUPLE

Do you find yourself going through a string of failed relationships while those around you all seem to be happy and content in their marriages? Do you ever stop to surprise what they are doing differently? Perhaps you have now found yourself with a partner you feel you could build a future with and want to do your best to make things last.

We have taken a look at behavioral traits that can damage relationships, but what about the behaviors that strengthen them? What are the secrets of those couples who have made their relationships last for twenty, thirty, forty years, or longer? Is it merely a case of learning to put up with your partner's challenging behaviors? Or is there much more to it?

Couples therapists agree there are several vital traits present in successful relationships that all couples should aspire to. Let's take a look:

Forgiving One Another

Developing the ability to forgive your partner freely is essential for developing when improving our relationship.

But what exactly does it mean to forgive deeply and freely? Many of us have never stopped to consider what forgiveness precisely entails. We think of it as a vague concept of letting go of wrongs committed against us, forgetting, and moving on. But true forgiveness is about far more than only moving on. Genuine pardoning includes not just relinquishing the wrongs done to you, however supplanting the hurt it caused with something positive, for example, getting sympathy, empathy, and, on account of our life partners, profound love.

Many of us have the incorrect belief that forgiving someone means allowing them to get away with whatever they did to us. But this is simply not the case. Forgiving someone does not mean we are not forgoing our need for justice, an apology, or reconciliation. Forgiveness is separate from the three things. For example, receiving an apology mean a person is necessarily forgiven. And forgiving a person does not mean we are obliged to reconcile with them. Forgiveness is a place we must come to independently of these three elements.

Another common misconception is that forgiveness is a sign of weakness, but this is simply not the case. True forgiveness can be immensely challenging to give and requires a great deal of inner strength. As I'm sure you will agree, this is as far as a weakness as one can get.

Forgiveness can be considered as having two elements; decisional and emotional. Decisional forgiveness occurs when we consciously move from ill will towards a person to wishing them well. We no longer wish for bad things to happen to the person who has hurt us, an essential first step on the journey. This is most often the most straightforward element of forgiveness to manage.

But emotional forgiveness goes much deeper. This type of forgiveness occurs when we can actively move away from the negative feelings the wrongdoing invoked in us and replace them with far more positive emotions. This part of forgiveness often takes time, as it is human nature to dwell on negative emotions, and even when we feel we have moved on, they tend to return when we least expect it. This is especially prevalent when our spouse has committed significant wrongdoing against us, such as telling lies or being unfaithful. Sometimes even the smallest trigger can lead us to recall events we thought we were over.

In all likelihood, you are mindful of the link between stress and physical ailments. Anxiety, worry, and resentment are linked to a wide range of illnesses. Chronic anger puts us into a constant fight-or-flight mode, which causes changes in heart rate, blood pressure, and immunity. But the good news is that there are also links between forgiveness and improved mental and physical health. When we forgive, we release the stress associated with our negative feelings, which leads to reduced anxiety, depression, and other mental illnesses.

Forgiving your partner for their wrongdoings also sends out a powerful message. When you do so, you make them aware that you know they did not intentionally set out to hurt you, as there is love between the two of you. This is an essential first step in letting your relationship mend.

Complimenting Your Partner

Regularly complimenting your partner is a simple way to show what you value in your loved one. It contributes to your spouse's positive self-esteem and provides a focus on all that is good about your relationship.

But while complimenting your partner when the two of you are alone is excellent, the relationship can be further strengthened by making these positive comments in front of others. And this needn't be a showy declaration of all that is wonderful about your spouse. Simple throwaway lines to friends and family such as "My husband made a great dinner last night" or "She always picks up the phone when I call" can go a long way to maintaining closeness and a sense of appreciation within a relationship.

Focusing on the Positives

All interactions have their ups and downs, even the strongest and most loving ones. But for a relationship to be happy and prosperous, the joyous moments must outweigh the negative. Successful couples make a habit of pointing out the positives within their relationship. They thank each other for kind words or actions, give compliments freely, and congratulate one another on their successes.

Similarly, couples tend to be stronger when they laugh a lot. This is a powerful trait that helps prevent life from becoming weighed down with stressors. Of course, all couples will face severe issues throughout their life, but being able to face challenges with a sense of humor can be a powerful asset.

Understanding Each Other's Differences

Most often, the cracks that form in a relationship are the result of two clashing personality types. We can easily interpret our partner's behavior as an attempt to create conflict or start an argument. But more often than not, disagreements arise because different personalities approach situations in different ways. Something we see as just a normal part of our day-to-day behavior may drive our partner mad; for example, if one habitually messy partner fails to put their clothes away at the end of the day. The tidy partner might misconstrue this as their loved one deliberately being lazy or disrespectful, while for the messy partner, it was merely a subconscious reaction with no deeper motive.

Successful couples invest time understanding who their partner is, what drives them, what irritates them, and what is important to them. When we progress a deeper understanding of our partner's inherent personality traits, we make it easier to avoid conflict and handle disagreements more effectively when they arise.

Expressing Interest in One Another's Lives

While you and your partner must have independent interests, one of the traits of successful couples is their ability to show interest in their partner's lives. It includes areas such as work-life, friendships, family, and hobbies. Ask questions regularly and listening intently to the answers.

This also goes a long way to assure you that you are comfortable with the part of their life that you are not involved in.

Letting Each Other Know When They Will Be Home

Of course, in any healthy relationship, there will be times when couples are apart. And a specific trait shared by many successful couples is that they consistently let their partner know when to expect them home. While it may seem petty or unnecessary, the simple act of calling or texting to let your partner know when you will back help build a sense of trust and security within a relationship and helps eliminate anxiety and worry.

Flirting With Each Other

Flirting is one of the keys to maintaining an active sex life and a connected and loving relationship outside the bedroom. Even and especially for couples who have been together for many years, flirting is a powerful way to show your attraction for your partner and keep the spark alive. When flirting is no longer present, the relationship runs the risk of becoming stale and mundane, both in and out of the bedroom.

Don't Fight Dirty

All couples fight, even the strongest ones. But those in successful relationships ensure that, when things get tense, they do not resort to name-calling, put-downs, or digging up the past. Even when you and your partner disagree, respecting one another is vital.

Developing Both Shared and Individual Interests

While successful couples have many things in common, they also have their interests. It is essential to develop shared hobbies and passions to thriving as a couple, but equally crucial to allow one another space to follow their interests.

To develop your shared interests, think back to what drew you to your partner in the first place. In all likelihood, you can pinpoint some things you have in common, which can develop into shared hobbies-if they have not done so already. These interests can be as simple as watching a movie together or as complicated as accompanying each other on the trip of a lifetime. Sharing interests and hobbies with your partner allows you to connect in new ways and create fresh memories of your lives together.

And when it comes to individual interests, successful couples make room for each other's unique hobbies and passions. They show an interest in each other's love, asking questions, and actively listening to the answer.

Going to Bed at the Same Time

Differences in schedules and sleeping patterns can make this a challenge for many couples. But to strengthen your relationship, try to adjust so you and your partner can go to bed at the same time several times a week. The act of falling asleep side by side while experiencing skin-to-skin contact is incredibly effective at strengthening a relationship's bonds.

Taking Time to Connect

Conversely, successful couples carve out time to truly connect, no matter how busy life gets, and no matter what is going on in the rest of the world or on their social media feeds. These moments of connection can be as simple as going for a walk, chatting over dinner, or even doing the dishes together. It's not the activity that's important. Instead, it's the fact that you set aside a specific time to be together.

CHAPTER 21: HOW TO DEAL WITH ANXIOUS ATTACHMENT AND JEALOUSY

One manifestation of insecurity is to be overly attached. There's nothing wrong with wanting to spend some time with our partner; actually, feeling connected to someone and demonstrating it is vital if you want to have a healthy and loving relationship. This becomes a problem when it's taken to an extreme. Being overly attached poses a danger to your relationship, and you need to learn how to manage this.

A person who's always being told what to do with the sole purpose of making the other happy has relinquished his own free will. His decisions and opinions are not considered because he has learned to leave it all to others to decide what's good for him. That person has become a puppet and has put his life in other's hands. He's as vulnerable as the other person wants him to be, and his self-worth is almost non-existent.

Even though this is usually an extreme case, this scenario repeats itself countless times. A relationship doesn't have to be like a prison, where one person feels he cannot move a single finger without consulting with the other whether it's right or not. Yes, there are certain circumstances where the mutual agreement will be necessary, but not all decisions in life require to be examined with an overly judgmental eye.

You're in no better position if you feel you're the one commanding. In a relationship, both will suffer. The one commanding and examining every movement is just showing how insecure he or she feels. The truth of the matter is that the relationship is not healthy. Just as an unreasonable boss is never satisfied with the explanations of his employee, the one demanding a constant explanation from his partner will never be quiet; rather, he'll be finding excuses not to believe any explanation.

A mother might think that she's shielding his son by maintaining him in a "bubble" where he is safe from threats, temptations, and danger. But the son will have to grow and mature. He will have to understand that life is also enjoyable outside the "bubble" where he was raised. By being overly attached to your partner, you might think you're protecting him from temptation or danger to your relationship, but you're just stifling his enjoyment of life. You're just making him wonder what it feels like to be outside of your relationship. In other words, by being overly attached, you're giving him more reasons to end the relationship.

A prisoner might reassure himself by thinking about the day when his release will come. Don't let your relationship be like a prison where your partner finds reassurance only when he thinks about the day when he leaves the relationship.

You Don't Possess Your Partner

By being overly attached, many people come to think that they have their partner. No human can be fully possessed by others. This goes against our desire to be and live free. A relationship is not the union of master and slave. Do you see your partner as someone who has to render an account to you? Do you feel like it's nothing less than a crime and an insult when he decides without consulting you? Why do you feel you have control over your partner?

If you think your partner has voluntarily come under your control by accepting being in a relationship, you have fooled yourself. Being in a relationship doesn't mean your partner has come to you to surrender all his rights and goals; it means he has come to you because he wants to share them with you. He has grown up to be a person who wants to share life moments with you, not for you to take them out of his hand, but to understand that he sees you as someone very special in his life.

The other way around is also true. You're being possessed by your partner if you're so attached to him that you want to follow everywhere he goes and supports every decision he makes just because you feel you have to be with him. Doing that might make you feel you're in a position of control; after all, you know what he's exactly doing, who he's been with, and where. But in reality, you're surrendering your freedom; you have left your decisions aside to follow your partner's. You've become possessed by your partner when all you wanted to do was to be sure he's been doing right.

Emotional Management

Do you feel like emotions can sometimes be overwhelming? Emotions are proof that we feel and can enjoy basic human experiences. When someone falls in love, he embarks on a roller coaster of emotions that might make him feel exhausted. Being in a relationship is not the end of that roller coaster. Although it provides a measure of security, you both still need to keep working if you want to make a success of this relationship.

Happiness and joy are normal feelings that follow after beginning a new relationship. But if you're an insecure person, these emotions soon turn into anger, frustration, or jealousy, but how? An insecure person will never be satisfied with her partner's reassurances whenever he makes a mistake or apologizes. Also, she might find it difficult to believe her partner.

Three Steps to Be Less Jealous and More Open to Listening

1. Realize your worth and avoid comparisons: You may not be perfect. You may not have the perfect body. But surely there's a lot your good at. Realize that you have a lot of value in the eyes of those closest to you. You have qualities that make you special to your partner, and those qualities set you apart as someone different, interesting, and attractive to your loved ones. With that being said, don't compare yourself to others! Do you feel that the fact that someone looks better than you or has better clothes than you make them a more important or better person than you? Outward appearances tend to matter little when choosing a life-long partner. Realize how much you're worth and continue working on your good qualities.
2. Try to get more involved with people: Spending time with people will yield great benefits for you and your relationship. Having an interest in others rather than yourself all the time will help you have more meaningful connections and will boost your self-esteem. The more you get to know people, the clearer you'll see that we all have the same problems and the less you'll worry about your insecurity. Do good things for others!
3. React to criticism in a proper way: Since we are all bound to make mistakes, it's only natural to expect that sooner or later, we will receive criticism. What matters here, though, is how you react to that criticism. Sure, there's criticism that's designed just to put you down. You can turn away and ignore it if you certainly realize that it is unfair, untrue, or diminishing. On the other hand, if the

criticism is well deserved, strive to listen to it and improve. An occasional mistake doesn't make you a failure as a person.

Striving to be a better person is not an easy task, but you can learn how to manage your emotions when you're confronted with criticism. Socializing will be a great tool in understanding how others see you, but remember that the closer we get, the easier it will be for you to see where your friends fall short, and they will see that about you too. Your good qualities already endear you to many people, especially to your partner! So, don't be afraid of showing them to the world!

CHAPTER 22: DON'T GET DISTRACTED BY TEMPTATIONS

After the initial stunning reaction, several feelings surface, frustration, fear, anxiety, uncertainty, resentment, desperation, and depression. All seems mixed up and somewhat surreal as if it were true for someone else, not for you. But it happens unexpectedly to you.

That is when you have to use every ounce of bravery and determination and a lot you haven't learned before. You have to build space immediately for some private time so that you can look after yourself, regroup, and develop an action plan.

You might have to take a day off from work, speak to a close friend, buy a diary, start writing your thoughts and feelings, or take a long walk in the park. Another choice is to make a therapy appointment and arrange it for you as soon as possible.

Then, spend some time thinking about how the situation should be handled. Your goal is to buy time so your wife does not run abruptly out of the house. You want to slow things down so that your wife can have the chance to reconsider and, if possible, agree to counsel you.

During this crisis, you will be the "guardian of the flame of marriage." It will be your duty to keep hope and love alive so that the fire will not burn out. You may say it's not fair, and it shouldn't be like this.

But in the final analysis, it is up to you to take constructive steps if you want to save your marriage, and your wife wants it. During the crisis, you must be prepared to do far more than just your fair share to keep your marriage together.

And that means giving your fears and anxieties, and it is up to you to keep hope alive - hope your marriage will do it-hope your partner changes his or her mind-hope your marriage can survive it and be even better than ever.

Here are some tips on how to keep hope thriving and manageable:

1. Don't give up on your marriage, irrespective of what your wife said. People change their minds sometimes. No condition is

impossible if at least one partner is prepared to do everything they need to maintain a marriage. There is always hope that through loving energy, your marriage can be transformed. Many spouses reconsider their original motivation to leave and continue to waste so much time and money only to throw away their marriage without at least seeking marriage advice.

2. Don't take what your wife says personally. People also say irrational things when they get angry or when they want to explain what they do. A wife who feels ashamed of telling you that she wants a divorce may get angry. A partner who never shared his true feelings about issues will eventually erupt through the years with a long list of faults.
3. Truly anchor in your mind that how you react to the situation has a significant influence on how things go from here. You give her the perfect reason to move ahead and get away if you keep criticizing a partner who needs emotional space. You can't control or not control what your wife wants to do, but you can control how you approach the situation.
4. Only claim that if your partner enquires what you are going to do subsequently, you're puzzled and need time to reflect; you don't want to make any hurried decisions. Being "disturbed" will disappoint a spouse who only waits to fight. It also keeps you for a bit.
5. Honor the emotional space application of your wife if that is a concern. Switch off and take some time to party, relax, and get your partner's spotlight off right now. If you allow your apprehension to take over and mandate instant responses to tough queries, you have to miss something.
6. List all the different things you can do to get mentally and physically more comfortable. Include exercise, yoga, biking or hiking, help close friends, hear motivational videos on the way to work, read books about people who have gone through tough times, gain encouragement from their spiritual roots and connections, attend services at your synagogue, temple or mosque or start individual therapy courses. Then prepare to incorporate what you think to be the most beneficial.
7. Decide that it is vital to you to know that whatever happens in your marriage, you gave it your most effective shot and that you

tried it all. Instead of trying to continuously grasp the likelihood that your marriage will succeed, put your effort into doing what you can in a supportive manner every day. Be constructive and behave positively.

8. Start to extend your life to include new interests and hobbies. Don't wait until everything has been resolved before you continue to enjoy your life as much as possible. Your marital situation may not be fixed, but that doesn't mean you have to evolve and worry continually. Extend yourself to enlarge your universe. You become more interesting as you enjoy yourself by engaging in things that interest you, including your partner.
9. Take a deliberate decision to stay optimistic and to expect something good and beneficial to emerge from this experience in the long term. Your intuition will affect what is going on. If you are skeptical, your actions will penetrate the strength of doubt. Tell yourself that a creative solution to every problem is always open-be confident in your ability to be imaginative, versatile, and resilient.

CHAPTER 23: HOW TO EASILY ADAPT TO CHANGE

If trouble or challenge comes in your path, when you are troubled and anxious, this is the time to put your trust in the Spirit, the Divine Presence, and to realize that now you can relax knowing that God is in charge of it. You should trust and trust that everything will be all right.

At the right time and in the perfect way, our success always comes to us. Our life keeps rising in perfect timing. As we learn to believe and trust in spiritual peace, we find that we can let go and allow our lives to work for us. We are much more valued than we would have expected. God is Divine Wisdom and resides in each one of us. We always have that wisdom at our fingertips. Know now that God wants for us everything good and perfect.

Be mindful that the critical step in learning to trust is to look carefully and attentively at your reactions. You don't have to criticize yourself or try to change your behavior. Only listen. What are the things you have had in the past? If you experience mistrust, where does it come from specifically? Once past feelings surface, you will have a better understanding of why trust is hard for you. This perspective is going to inspire change.

Trust yourself. A great deal of mistrust of others is the incapacity to trust others. The subconscious minds assume responsibility when someone harms or betrays us. I was stupid enough to believe them. It's my fault. While it's true that we co-create our world, the reality is that many things are beyond our control. Forgiving and believing in our actions is a fundamental aspect of maintaining faith in others. Simple statements are a high starting point. In a reflective position, think or say to yourself. "I trust in myself. I trust in my ability to make the right decisions. I trust in the world to lead me to where I need to go." Repeat such statements as often as possible using whatever terms and strategies.

Find your natural state. We trust life entirely in our hearts. We know that we're on the right path for us already. Yet, our mental and spiritual powers don't always share this feeling. Restore faith is a matter of linking our hearts and opening up in us the root of love. We instinctively want to feel satisfied, secure, and willing to trust others, whether in the bedroom or the boardroom. It may take compassion, validation, and good old-fashioned hard work, but it's invaluable to be able to trust again.

CONCLUSION

Watching a relationship that you have invested your emotions, time, and energy into going down the drain can be heartbreaking. Most couples go through ups and downs in the process of trying to get to know each other and trying to build a life together. Understanding what causes these differences and uncovering your hidden insecurities is the most effective way to overcome anxiety and build lasting relationships.

Love is often not enough to sustain a relationship. Trust, intimacy, openness, a willingness to compromise, and secure attachment are also required if a relationship is to succeed. Just like it takes two people to make a healthy relationship, it also takes two people to break a relationship.

A willingness to recognize the role we play in our relationships creates the room we need for improvement. When it comes down to building a healthy relationship, there is no room for blaming and scapegoating. Start by accepting that you are equally responsible for what is going on in your relationship. Then start working towards a better future together.

This book aims to equip you with the necessary information and tools to build a healthier relationship. The strategies provided herein are meant to be practical and easy to follow no matter what stage your relationship is in. It could be months, years, or decades old, but the ingredients for a healthy relationship are constant for any of these stages.

The importance of communication, conflict resolution, emotionally focused therapy, and many other pertinent topics relating to relationships have all been covered comprehensively in this book. We hope that your understanding of the dynamics of your relationship is now much better than when you started reading this book.

You have already taken the first step to creating a healthy relationship by reading this book. The next step is to start applying the principles described in this text. Start small and implement changes gradually at a pace that is manageable for you and your partner. Remember, you can adopt the strategies that seem better suited for your relationship and leave the rest for when you need them.

Love does indeed make the world go around, but you need to create a solid enough foundation to support the love in your relationship. Do not leave the fate of your relationship up to destiny. You have been empowered to take charge of your relationship and make it what you want it to be.

It is my sincere hope that this book will help you improve your relationship.

www.ingramcontent.com/pod-product-compliance
Lightning Source LLC
LaVergne TN
LVHW022101200926
848481LV00003B/1015
* 9 7 9 8 2 1 5 8 3 7 8 4 9 *